Quarterly Essay

Quarterly Essay is published four times a year by Black Inc., an imprint of Schwartz Books Pty Ltd. Publisher: Morry Schwartz.

ISBN 9781863959704 ISSN 1832-0953

Subscriptions – 1 year print & digital (4 issues): $79.95 within Australia incl. GST. Outside Australia $119.95. 2 years print & digital (8 issues): $149.95 within Australia incl. GST. 1 year digital only: $49.95.

Payment may be made by Mastercard or Visa, or by cheque made out to Schwartz Books. Payment includes postage and handling.

To subscribe, fill out and post the subscription form inside this issue, or subscribe online:

quarterlyessay.com
subscribe@blackincbooks.com
Phone: 61 3 9486 0288

Correspondence should be addressed to:

The Editor, Quarterly Essay
Level 1, 221 Drummond Street
Carlton VIC 3053 Australia
Phone: 61 3 9486 0288 / Fax: 61 3 9011 6106
Email: quarterlyessay@blackincbooks.com

Editor: Chris Feik. Management: Elisabeth Young. Publicity: Anna Lensky. Design: Guy Mirabella Assistant Editor: Kirstie Innes-Will. Production Coordinator: Marilyn de Castro. Typesetting: Akiko Chan.

Printed in Australia by McPherson's Printing Group. The paper used to produce this book comes from wood grown in sustainable forests.

RED FLAG

Waking up to China's challenge

Peter Hartcher

We hear a great deal about the power and might of the risen China and the man sometimes called its "ruler for life," President Xi Jinping. But what does the supreme ruler of China want to do with all this power? Only knowing that can we comprehend where Australia fits into his plan.

We know some of Xi's grand aims for his nation. And we know his big taboos, too. He has declared the pursuit of the "China Dream" to be the overarching ambition of his time. The dream, he says, is the "rejuvenation of the great Chinese nation." Xi is clear about what his dream includes. Such as being a "moderately well-off society" by 2021. He doesn't specify, but if you apply the informal rule of thumb that defines a middle-income country as having US$10,000 in income per head annually, China is on track to surpass this a year or two early, putting it in the same income league as Malaysia and Russia by the end of 2019. And Xi dreams of a fully rich China by 2049, the centenary of Mao Zedong's founding of the People's Republic. The country will be "closer to centre-stage" of world affairs, in Xi's vision. This refers to China's ancient name for itself – the two characters that are sometimes translated as "Middle Kingdom" can also be rendered "Central Kingdom."

A fond fantasy? Not at all. China's economy was the biggest in the world for at least half a millennium, until as recently as 1820. It is not inevitable that it will vault over the United States to recover that title, but it is likely, and likely by about the time today's newborns are ready to start high school. It's a distinction without much of a difference. China will have about the same economic heft as the US, maybe a bit more, maybe a bit less. But whichever it is, it is already well advanced towards superpower status, its economy as big as those of the entire European Union and Japan put together. Economic bulk is the base feedstock of national power. Even at today's subdued growth rate, China's economy is adding so much new activity that it's "growing" another Australia every two years.

Imperial China, a world leader in technology, also pioneered the capable, modern nation-state. It took Europe almost two millennia to catch up. China is again thrusting to the forefront of technological know-how and pioneering a more effective nation-state. For instance, in less than half the time Australia has spent debating inconclusively whether to build a single fast rail line to connect its major cities, China built a network of over 20,000 kilometres of fast rail.

Its return to imperial-era greatness has many modern touches. To keep the kids connected to the spirit of nation-building, China's gaming behemoth, Tencent, launched a new game. Patriotically titled *Homeland Dream*, it went live just in time for celebrations of the seventieth anniversary of the founding of the People's Republic this year. As described by *The Financial Times*, the game "allows players to build virtual cities filled with Communist slogans and landmarks." It went instantly to the top of the list of most popular games. "For China's biggest video game company, a patriotic business strategy appears to be paying off." Unpatriotic ones are less likely to succeed. Every new game needs the approval of the state. And for lovers of liberty who fret over China's tech-enhanced surveillance and control – the US-based independent watchdog organisation Freedom House has dubbed the game "techno-dystopian expansionism" – China has become hyper-capable in a troubling way.

The spirit of the once-mighty empire that built the Great Wall and the Great Canal is taking concrete form once more with Beijing's imperial-scale ambition for its vast intercontinental Belt and Road scheme for connecting the world through Chinese money and power. The Central Kingdom has every prospect of being much "closer to centre-stage," just as Xi wishes.

And by the same date of 2049, he sees Beijing "recovering" the self-governing democratic island of Taiwan for the Chinese Communist Party (CCP), a prospect that troubles most of Taiwan's 24 million people. It's no coincidence that Hong Kong's special autonomy under the "One Country, Two Systems" formula is due to expire in the same year.

That's what Xi wants. A country as rich as the richest on earth, with all its territories united under the centralised rule of the CCP, in a magnificent restoration of China's sovereign splendour before it was torn apart by British, European and Japanese forces after 1842. That was the beginning of what China calls its "century of humiliation." Xi's dream is to end the ignominy in glory.

Xi intends to be nothing less than a threshold figure in world history. The Soviet Communist Party collapsed because "in the end nobody was a real man," Xi said in his first months in power. Implicitly, he was asserting that only a "real man" could hold China together. He was that man. The iron fist had announced itself. There would be no ideological wavering or political timidity. He changed China's constitution, removing term limits for the leader, so he could rule indefinitely.

Xi has the benign appearance of a kindly uncle. One of his nicknames is Winnie the Pooh. But he is the most repressive Chinese leader since Mao. Inside China's Great Firewall, official censors scrub the web of any such ursine reference. Not only is anything so disrespectful unacceptable, it might be used as a coded reference to circumvent the strict ban on criticism of the president. Disney's harmless 2018 movie *Christopher Robin*, plainly a subversive Western attempt to undercut the power of the CCP, was banned. In truth, Xi is more grizzly bear than Pooh.

The leader went further. Not content to assert unassailable power at home, he overturned the famous maxim that had guided China's overarching strategy for almost a quarter-century. Paramount leader Deng Xiaoping in 1990 urged restraint on a China that was beginning to pulse with the possibilities of its own rising power. Deng urged his compatriots to "hide your brightness, bide your time." Xi declared that China was now "striving to achieve." This is a crystallising statement of China's transformation. It was a status quo power. It's now an ambitious one. Barack Obama accused China under Xi of using "sheer size and muscle to force countries into subordinate positions."

We also know what Xi doesn't want. In a secret directive that became famous as Document No. 9 after it was exposed by a Chinese journalist, Xi laid down what have become known as the "seven taboos" or "seven unmentionables" for today's China. It was written in the first six months of Xi's rule and issued by the General Office of the Central Committee of the Communist Party of China, which Xi, of course, leads. It demanded "intense struggle" against seven "false trends."

The first taboo is "Western constitutional democracy." It is denounced as a vessel for "capitalist class concepts." First among them is the separation of powers. This is the doctrine that puts checks on power, so that one branch of government can check another. Its purpose is to prevent the rise of a tyrant, to protect the rights of citizens.

A practical example is that, in a liberal democracy, a citizen can challenge a government decision in court. But Xi's Document No. 9 encyclical specifically denounces "independent judiciaries." So too multi-party systems, general elections and "nationalised armies." What does this peculiar term mean? In normal countries, the army serves the state, regardless of which party happens to be in power. But in China it is fully owned and controlled by the Chinese Communist Party. As Mao said: "The principle is that the party commands the gun, and the gun must never be allowed to command the party." The army and the courts are not national institutions. They are partisan. They serve the party, and only the party.

Second, the concept of "universal values" is forbidden. The first of the universal values promulgated by the United Nations is a fundamental one: that "All human beings are born free and equal in dignity and rights." Xi rejects it. He regards it to be a challenge to the rule of the Chinese Communist Party. The party recognises collective rights – to development and security, for instance – while rejecting individual rights, such as to vote, to speak freely and to worship.

Third, civil society is taboo. That is, any community-based body or non-government organisation, like a charity, environmental group, trade union, professional group or church, is forbidden. Document No. 9 says that "advocates of civil society want to squeeze the party out of leadership of the masses at the local level" and constitute a "serious form of political opposition." So organisations like Falun Gong, or Falun Dafa, are brutally repressed. Religions, always strictly controlled in modern China, increasingly are persecuted under Xi. The repression of China's Uighur Muslims, with a million or more detained indefinitely in mass camps from 2017 and denied the right to practise their beliefs, is a dramatic escalation.

Fourth, neoliberalism is a no-no. The doctrine of unrestrained market forces is the US-led Western world's attempt to "change China's basic economic system ... under the guise of globalisation" and "weaken the government's control of the national economy." It should be noted that, since Document No. 9 was first drawn up, the United States under Donald Trump has ceased to advocate neoliberalism, which now stands friendless in the world.

Fifth, the West's idea of journalism is unmentionable. Why? Because it is "challenging China's principle that the media and publishing system should be subject to party discipline." Freedom of the press is a "pretext" for challenging the Marxist definition of news. The media is not "society's public instrument" but should be "infused with the spirit of the party."

Sixth, historical nihilism is banned. The document says that historical nihilism is "trying to undermine the history of the Chinese Communist Party and of New China." "In the guise of 'reassessing history'," says the encyclical, historical nihilism is "tantamount to denying the legitimacy of the Chinese Communist Party's long-term political dominance."

Finally, questioning reform and opening and the socialist nature of "socialism with Chinese characteristics" is forbidden. "The discussion of reform has been unceasing," says the paper. "Some views clearly deviate from socialism with Chinese characteristics." Decoded, this simply means that further major economic reform is off-limits and should not be discussed.

So Document No. 9, or, more formally, the Communiqué on the Current State of the Ideological Sphere, has three striking characteristics. First, its unwavering theme is the imperative of party control above all else. Second, its psychological stance is defensive, even paranoid. Each of the central principles of Western civilisation is dismissed as "pretext" or a "guise" or a "political tool" for undermining the Chinese Communist Party. Third, it is a directive to all party cadres to snuff out the fundamental values and liberties at the heart of liberal democracy. It is hostile to the essence and the governing principles of societies such as Australia's. It defines the party's ideological sphere as directly opposed to the West's.

How do we know that Document No. 9 is authentic? One indication is that, while it was not publicised, it was posted on some Chinese government websites. Another is that the journalist who first published the document outside officialdom, Gao Yu, was arrested for publishing state secrets, forced to make a televised "confession," and jailed, initially for seven years, later amended to house arrest with a reduced sentence of five years due to her poor health. Gao is seventy-five years old. Her treatment suggests that the party is not proud of its declaration of the seven perils. China puts great effort into projecting a positive image to the world. Its public pronouncements gush about peace, humanity and the boast that "China always attaches great importance to human rights," as it claimed in its declaration to the United Nations General Assembly in September. A third indication is that its precepts have since been disseminated in compulsory study sessions, some of which have been documented on the internet. Corporate managers, university administrators and other officials have been instructed in the seven taboos. Finally, Document No. 9 has been enforced, the ultimate validation of its authenticity.

This is the China of Xi's dreams, in his own words. Rich, more central in world affairs, united under one unchallengeable party, vigilantly stamping out any freedom, justice or human right that might crimp the power of the party. It is to be, in other words, an authoritarian superpower. Can Australia live with it? Can Australia live without it?

Standing to give the toast at a lunch in the chandeliered ballroom of a Sydney hotel, China's First Vice Premier raised his glass of wine to the hundreds of businesspeople before him. "Let's all get rich together!" exclaimed Zhu Rongji with a broad grin, to the delight of his audience. It was 1997, and it was not only the wine that was intoxicating.

Zhu was about to become premier of China, and China was about to become a full member of the global market system through admission to the World Trade Organization. The Soviet Union was a memory. It was difficult to reconcile Zhu's unabashed capitalist gloating with the name of the political group pursuing it, the Chinese Communist Party. Communism seemed such an anachronism. It was almost embarrassing to say the word. Zhu wore not a Mao suit but a business suit, talked more like Gordon Gekko than Karl Marx. The country's growth had been impressive. It was about to become explosive.

At the moment that the businesspeople in the room laughed and clinked glasses at the sheer audacity of Zhu's toast, China's economy was roughly twice the size of Australia's. Just as it had been when Australia first extended diplomatic recognition to Beijing in 1972. The ratio − two to one − had not changed in a quarter-century. But by 2018, China's economy was nearly ten times the size of Australia's.

China's take-off was not unprecedented in its speed. Japan grew at similarly breakneck rates in its early decades after World War II. Nor was China's growth unprecedented in its duration. Japan's post-war boom ran about as long. What set China apart was sheer scale. With 1.4 billion people, China contains almost a fifth of humanity. Taken together, the speed, duration and scale of the transformation was truly one of the wonders of the modern world.

Two specifics can help us appreciate the abstract. First, China used more cement between 2011 and 2013 than the United States used in the entire twentieth century. "It's a statistic so mind-blowing that it stunned Bill Gates and inspired haiku," wrote a *Washington Post* reporter. Second, China's growth lifted 850 million people out of absolute poverty in the four decades to 2013. That was the population of planet Earth until the nineteenth century. The World Bank observes that, of all the people in the world who managed to escape poverty in the last four decades, seven of every ten were Chinese. It describes this as "unprecedented in scope and scale." Or, in the words of China's government, "a miracle in the development of mankind."

Zhu's toast was no delusion. Along the way, Australia and China did get rich together. China displaced all other trading partners to become Australia's biggest export market. China buys a third of everything that Australia sells to the world. That's double the share of the next biggest market, Japan. The last time Australia was so dependent on one country for its income was in the 1950s, when it was a client state of Britain.

For a sense of China's preponderance, consider this: Chinese tourists spend about $11 billion a year in Australia. Australia earns about the same, $11 billion a year, by attracting Chinese students to its universities and colleges. Either one of these individual lines of business with China is more valuable than the entirety of Australia's exports to the United Kingdom. China is the biggest overseas buyer for both Australian industries.

Still, as valuable as those services trades are to Australia, they pale in comparison to the resources business. The sale of rocks accounts for 53 cents in every dollar of total Australian sales to China. That's mostly iron ore, but includes coal, bauxite and other ores. Add other raw materials, such as gas and wool and beef and barley and lobsters, and almost three-quarters of Australia's total exports to China are raw products, feeding the Chinese industrial machine as well as its banquet tables and households.

China's appetites are so voracious that it doesn't just wait to see what Australian exporters might offer to sell. An industry of citizen exporters sprang up to satisfy its needs, filling their shopping trolleys with Australian baby formula, vitamins and skincare products and then mailing them to increasingly discerning retail customers in China. This trade is operated by around 150,000 Chinese students and tourists and other residents in Australia, known as *daigou*, a term that translates as "buy on behalf of." Its estimated sales are $2.5 billion a year, according to a company that helps service the *daigou*, AuMake. Sales that corporate Australia was too slow or too complacent to pursue are made by enterprising individual Chinese. Even sailors with the Chinese navy joined the rush. The crews of three Chinese naval ships on a port visit to Sydney in June 2019 were photographed carting vanloads of baby formula onto their warships to take home.

"China remains the key growth opportunity for many Australian companies despite a slowing economy and more regulatory risk," Stewart Oldfield of market intelligence firm Field Research writes in *The Australian Financial Review*. "Australia–China trade has continued to grow strongly over the past two years despite tensions. Two-way goods trade expanded by 17.5 per cent in 2018, five times faster than global trade growth, topping $192 billion. Australian-listed company exposure to China goes well beyond its traditional strengths in iron ore and coal and these days includes infant formula, education and employment services, pharmaceuticals, fruit, wine and tourism."

There are many tales of woe, but a company or industry that successfully catches the China market updraft feels like it's gone from climbing the stairs to zooming skywards in a high-speed elevator. Wine, for instance. A decade ago Australia sold 3 million cases to China a year, worth $120 million. Today it's gone to 17 million cases, fetching $1.1 billion and displacing the French wine industry as the biggest supplier to China.

The Reserve Bank of Australia has "more staff looking at China than any other single overseas economy," according to its governor, Philip Lowe, even though the United States is still by far the larger of the two. So why devote more resources to studying China? Partly because of the opportunities. Casting ahead to 2030, the Australian Treasury forecasts that the total size of the US economy will be US$24 trillion. Which sounds impressive until you see that it projects China's to be US$42 trillion, 175 per cent the size of America's.

Of course, it is merely a forecast. Many over the past twenty years did falsely predict a collapse of China's economy, but have been so worn down by being so wrong for so long that most have given up. That does not mean a Chinese economic shock is impossible. As he prepared to retire in 2017, China's then central bank chief, Zhou Xiaochuan, stunned markets with the bluntness of a warning that "we should particularly defend against" a "sharp correction, what we call a 'Minsky moment.'" A sudden collapse in asset prices like real estate and shares, in other words. China has not repealed the laws of economics, but has managed to navigate them success-fully for far longer than most Western analysts would have credited. And this is another reason that Australia's Reserve Bank devotes more resources to China-watching — because of the risks. "Among the largest economic risks that Australia faces is something going wrong in China," said the gov-ernor. Or, as business commentator Robert Gottliebsen put it: "We are incredibly dependent on China — in some ways we are a state of China."

And a final reason is because of the peculiarities. Lowe mentioned some of these, foremost that Australia and China have "different political sys-tems." The differences needed extra effort to comprehend, he said.

As a country with enormous exposure to a great power with a funda-mentally different system, Australia's essential starting point is to ask: what does China want from the world? And, specifically, what does China want from Australia?

*

For Joe Hockey, the realisation hit him while he was sitting in a traditional thatched hut in Bali. After only two days as treasurer, he was utterly unpre-pared for his meeting with China's finance minister. It was September 2013, and Hockey was representing Australia at a meeting of the twenty-one Asia-Pacific Economic Cooperation countries.

Chinese officials had shuttled back and forth to the hut for hours finess-ing every detail, but when Lou Jiwei strode in, sat down opposite Hockey and blithely lit a cigarette, it wasn't detail that concerned him. "So," Lou opened by saying, "why won't you let me buy Rio Tinto?" Rio is one of the world's great mining companies. It draws high-quality iron ore, bauxite, diamonds, gold, copper and uranium from its mines in Australia, Canada, Mongolia and elsewhere. Although it's only part-Australian, with dual headquarters in London and Melbourne, it is one of Australia's proudest corporate assets.

China had made a 2008 bid through a state-owned firm to buy 15 per cent of the company. Beijing was anxious to lock down the raw materials to feed its vast industrial appetites. The global financial crisis was under-way, so it was going cheap. The Rudd government approved the sale, but made clear that 15 per cent was the maximum stake for a state-owned foreign investor. Now, four years on, Lou Jiwei wanted to revisit the idea.

"That's fine," Hockey parried once he'd recovered from his surprise. "As long as you'll let Qantas buy China Southern," a state-owned airline, the biggest in Asia. Lou didn't like that idea. He tried another angle: "All I want," he told Hockey through an interpreter, "is to buy 15 per cent of your top 200 listed companies." The Australian treasurer's response was to laugh at the brazenness of the proposal. If granted, it would make the Chinese government the biggest single investor in corporate Australia. In many companies it would make the Chinese government the most influential shareholder. And, overall, it would give the Chinese government unmatched sway over the conduct of companies, industries, banks, financial markets, regulators and governments.

When the brash former head of China's sovereign wealth fund saw that this wasn't going to be accepted, he put another idea to Hockey. Lou suggested Chinese buyers could take major stakes in Australia's big banks. Hockey didn't countenance this, either. Rather than allow Lou to work through a list of options for acquiring broad ownership of Australia's corporate crown jewels, Hockey suggested they move on to a "more meaningful" topic.

The encounter stunned Hockey. It revealed several important aspects of the Chinese government's intent and conduct. First, Lou put aside any pretence that state-owned companies act independently of the Chinese Communist Party. It was clear that he expected to direct the behaviour of Chinese state-owned firms. Second, Lou's proposals were a naked play to use the resources of the Chinese system to buy the maximum possible ownership, and, with that, the maximum possible power and influence over Australia. There was nothing said about investment returns or business profitability. Lou was interested in ownership for its own sake. Third was the sheer brazenness of the bid. It revealed towering arrogance and raw hubris. What did China want from Australia? As much power and influence over its economy as it could get. It's possible that Lou had no real expectation that such an abrupt and ambitious bid would be considered seriously. If so, we can only assume that he hoped to awe the new Australian treasurer with his power. In the event, a Chinese state-owned firm did manage to buy a slice of Rio, its coalmining business. Yancoal bought full ownership of Coal & Allied from Rio for $3.5 billion in 2017.

*

For Stephen Conroy, it hit him in a phone call from someone he'd thought was on his side. Conroy, a Labor senator and Victorian powerbroker, was the shadow defence minister. He took a call from the general secretary of the NSW Labor Party, Kaila Murnain. It was 17 June 2016, and a federal election was due in just fourteen days.

"Steve, if you don't change your China position, we are going to lose $400,000" in a promised political donation, she told him, according to the account that a shocked Conroy gave to many of his colleagues at the time. The timing gave it extra potency. The sudden loss of such a big pledge so close to an election could punch a hole in the party's final ad campaign, maybe even a decisive one. He added his interpretation: "This is serious when they can manipulate us two weeks out from an election."

For a political party, that is a huge sum. The public hearings of the NSW Independent Commission Against Corruption this year revealed that

NSW Labor was prepared to break the law and engage in elaborate cover-ups to get its hands on a donation one-quarter as big during a state campaign. In 2019, Murnain lost her job over that scandal.

Curiously, it was the same donor, the property tycoon and billionaire Huang Xiangmo, behind both offers, according to evidence to the ICAC on the state campaign and according to multiple Labor sources on the federal. For the record, he has denied being the donor on either occasion.

A donation of $400,000 would have been among the biggest donations from any individual in Australian political history. Huang was a permanent resident of Australia and lived in a $12.8-million home in Sydney's Mosman, which he's been forced to abandon. The Australian government has since cancelled his visa and declared him a persona non grata after ASIO found him to be a covert agent of influence for the CCP.

The "China position" that was so upsetting that Huang would offer $400,000 to change it? The previous day, Conroy had debated the defence minister, Marise Payne, at the National Press Club as part of the election campaign. In the course of debate, Conroy declared that a Labor government would take a firmer stand in resisting Chinese encroachments on its neighbours' territorial claims in the hotly contested South China Sea. "The Turnbull government has hidden behind ambiguous language," said Conroy. "We believe our defence force should be authorised to conduct freedom-of-navigation operations consistent with international law."

Conroy refused to alter his position. Murnain's reaction? "Ms Murnain is said to have been seen in Labor head office cursing about losing 'hundreds of thousands' of dollars worth of donations after Victorian Stephen Conroy made utterances on Labor's policy on the South China Sea," according to a report in *The Australian*.

What Huang failed to buy in the wholesale market he decided to shop for in the retail market instead. He quickly organised for another Labor senator, Sam Dastyari, to declare a more Beijing-friendly position. Dastyari wasn't a relevant frontbencher, so his words wouldn't carry the same weight, but he was a Labor powerbroker nonetheless, with solid influence in the NSW Right faction, which is often at odds with Conroy's faction in the Victorian Right. Better to have at least some of the federal Opposition spouting your favoured policy than none at all.

That same day, Dastyari called a press conference and, standing side by side with Huang, said that "the South China Sea is China's own affair," and that Australia should "respect China's decision." Only Chinese-language media were invited. When challenged by Australian reporters over his reported comments, Dastyari denied them. Until an audio recording emerged. Dastyari had been a cheerful recipient of Huang's cash for some time. A key point here: he had disclosed the money he'd taken from Huang. It was all legal. Property developers, such as Huang, are prohibited from giving money at the state level, but not at the federal. Dastyari was drummed out of federal parliament in disgrace, not for accepting Huang's money but for dissembling over the favours he was doing for him. It might have been legal, but it was plainly corrupt.

The first lesson from this episode is how cheap it is to buy Australian politics. When Huang Xiangmo wanted to have a bit of a flutter, he gambled hundreds of millions of dollars a year at one casino alone. We know from a 2015 leaked internal email from Melbourne's Crown Casino that Huang put nearly $800 million through its tables in one year. By comparison, the donations Huang offered political parties to change policy, and potentially compromise themselves, were mere pocket change. It exposes an extremely uneven contest. A desperate, low-rent political system has grave difficulty resisting the temptations offered by an extraordinarily well-funded influence-seeking operation. To illustrate, someone with Huang's play-money allowance could donate ten times the combined advertising spend of both major parties at the 2019 election and still have half a billion dollars in his pocket to splash on Crown Casino's games of chance. And Huang was just one covert agent of influence, according to ASIO.

Second, this incident jolted Australia into realising how little it knew of the Chinese government's covert influence campaign. When I first disclosed that Labor had been offered $400,000 to change its policy on the South China Sea, my colleague Nick McKenzie, an investigative reporter for *The Age* and *The Sydney Morning Herald*, was alarmed. It was the impetus, he says, for his decision to pursue a major 2017 investigation of China's influence operations in Australia. The series, in conjunction with the ABC's Chris Uhlmann and *Four Corners*, was a key moment in waking Australia to the operation. And we only received this warning because Conroy refused the offer and let his colleagues know about it. How many other such proposals have been made and silently accepted? In truth, we have no idea and no systemic way of finding out.

The intelligence agency whose primary job is to guard against foreign interference, ASIO, has only a limited idea. Covert foreign intrusion into the heart of Australian politics is "something we need to be very, very careful about," the recently retired head of ASIO, Duncan Lewis, says in an interview. "One spectacular case in New South Wales was Sam Dastyari. It's quite clear to me that any person in political office is potentially a target. I'm not trying to create paranoia, but there does need to be a level of sensible awareness. When people talked about [how to define foreign interference in] our political system, I used to get the comment, 'We will know it if we see it.' But not necessarily. Not if it's being done properly. There would be some I don't know about."

The Australian system is wide open in two critical ways. First, because "federally, Australia has some of the most lax political donations laws in the developed world," in the words of a senior lecturer in politics at the University of New South Wales, Lindy Edwards. The political donation laws are "full of holes that can be exploited to hide where parties' incomes are really coming from." She calculates that the major parties disclose transparently only 10 to 20 per cent of their true incomes as donations. And, second, because Australia has no federal anti-corruption commission. The system is dark, and there is no agency whose job it is to shine a light.

*

For three top leaders of the federal Labor Party – Penny Wong, Bill Shorten and Richard Marles – it hit them in a meeting with a top Chinese official. Meng Jianzhu was visiting Sydney in April 2017 and asked to meet the Opposition leader. Meng was a member of the Politburo, meaning that he was one of the twenty-five most senior members of the Chinese Communist Party. Shorten invited Wong, Labor's foreign affairs spokesperson, and Marles, defence spokesperson, to the meeting at the Commonwealth Parliamentary Offices in Bligh Street.

Beijing's biggest priority at the time was to get Australia to approve an extradition treaty. The Chinese government argued that corrupt officials were fleeing and hiding in Australia. Beijing wanted the ability to extract them to face charges in China.

It was true that officials had fled in the face of Xi's vast and zealous anti-corruption campaign. In six years of Xi's campaign to catch "tigers and flies" – major figures as well as minor ones – the CCP and state authorities punished 1.5 million people, many of whom were purged from the party, meaning an end to privilege and the onset of hardship. Of these, 58,000 were prosecuted in the court system and two sentenced to death. Among them were some of the very biggest creatures in the Chinese jungle, including cabinet-level officials, top party bosses and two dozen senior generals. According to China's media, one general had collected so much ill-gotten cash, gold and antiques that it took ten army transport trucks to remove it all. The other key aspect of the campaign that's been commonly observed by China-watchers is that while probably most of the people accused were indeed guilty of corruption, everyone accused was certainly guilty of belonging to the wrong political faction.

It was just such a treaty that pitched Hong Kong into this year's convulsive street protests. As the people of Hong Kong well know, there is no rule of law in mainland China, only rule by politics. There is no independent judiciary, so there can be no guarantee of fairness. Millions have márched against Hong Kong's proposed treaty with Beijing. They do not want to allow the CCP easy reach into the city, to pluck people out and disappear them into China's prosecution and prison system.

But in 2017 Australia's government supported the idea of an extradition treaty with the People's Republic of China and had already negotiated the text. It just needed parliamentary approval. Meng, in charge of all law enforcement in China as secretary of the Central Political and Legal Affairs Commission, wanted to get Labor on board to ensure smooth passage. But when he met some resistance from the Labor trio, Meng shocked them. He threatened them.

"It would be a shame if Chinese government representatives had to tell the Chinese community in Australia that Labor did not support the relationship between Australia and China," he said, according to a report by *The Australian*'s Primrose Riordan and later confirmed by participants independently. It was a threat to mobilise the 1.2 million ethnic Chinese people living in Australia against Labor.

The threat was counterproductive. Meng had shown the Labor leadership the ugly face of political coercion. It alarmed them. It confirmed Labor's concerns about exposing people in Australia to the CCP's reach. Labor's position only hardened. "I decline to change my position," Shorten replied, according to people present at the meeting. Labor opposed the extradition treaty. The treaty was now a dead letter. Meng reached retirement age later that same year and no longer holds office.

There are three key elements of the incident. First, a top member of the Chinese leadership thought it acceptable to threaten an Australian political party with political reprisal. Second, he was prepared to intervene directly in Australian domestic politics, using the power of the Chinese state to favour one party against another to get his way. These two facts offend the principle of non-interference in another sovereign country, a principle that the Chinese government always preaches, but is revealed here not to practise. Third, he represented the Chinese ethnic population of Australia as a national political asset of China that can be mobilised by Chinese government representatives. This presumption is false: some ethnic Chinese residents of Australia do give higher allegiance to their country of origin than to their country of residence, but a great many do not. Meng, and any Chinese mainland official who lays claim to their loyalty, does all Chinese Australians great harm.

This assertion that Beijing somehow has the ultimate claim on all ethnic Chinese people's loyalties is based on a racist premise. It's this: it doesn't matter where you were born, where you live, where you want your children to grow up, where you choose to invest your life and your loyalty, or which country gives you citizenship, you are ethnic Chinese and your race transcends all else – including your own free will. That immutable predetermination is the very definition of racism.

The Chinese Communist Party doesn't present this as a matter of choice. It's not a question of Chinese Australians feeling residual affection for China, which would be quite natural. It's a matter of compulsion according to official policy. There are some 60 million ethnic Chinese living in about 180 countries worldwide. Of these, about 80 per cent are citizens of the countries that they live in. But a teaching manual published by the CCP's United Front Work Department, the department of the Chinese government tasked with organising the Chinese populations overseas covertly to serve its strategic interests, states: "The unity of Chinese at home requires the unity of the sons and daughters of Chinese abroad." It exhorts its cadres to emphasise "flesh and blood" ties to the motherland. The manual, titled *China United Front Course Book*, isn't in general circulation but was obtained by London's *Financial Times* in 2017. The claim to enforced racial loyalty is supplemented with instruction on how it should be aided by "providing funding or other resources to selected overseas Chinese groups and individuals deemed valuable to Beijing's cause," in the words of the FT. This undercuts the standing and trust that the entire Chinese Australian population enjoys in Australia. When an immigrant decides to take up citizenship, he or she gives this oath: "I pledge my loyalty to Australia and its people, whose democratic beliefs I share, whose rights and liberties I respect, and whose laws I will uphold and obey." In laying claim to the eternal soul of every ethnic Chinese person, Meng and the party he represents seek to make every Australian Chinese person who has taken this vow into a liar at best and a traitor at worst.

*

For Feng Chongyi, it hit him when he saw the advertisements for a pair of concerts. They were billed as "Red Songs" to celebrate Chairman Mao Zedong. One concert was to be held at Sydney Town Hall and another at Melbourne Town Hall. They were scheduled for September 2016, to mark the fortieth anniversary of the death of the founder of the People's Republic of China. The problem, of course, is that the leader known as the "Great Helmsman" was also a great purveyor of death.

"It immediately caught our attention," says Feng, an associate professor of China studies at the University of Technology Sydney. "The idea of a Mao concert would be controversial even in China itself because it's a symbol of the Cultural Revolution, which reminds people of the nightmare of horrible suffering and persecution. Especially for the people who came to Australia to escape persecution in China." After Mao's disastrous Great Leap Forward created a man-made famine that killed anywhere from 18 million to 56 million people, he recovered political control with the violent purge known as the Cultural Revolution, which killed millions more. In engineering these great convulsions, Mao was responsible for more deaths than any other leader in history.

But the glorification of Mao in the great civic gathering places of Australia's two principal cities didn't seem to strike anyone outside the Chinese community as odd. The two town halls took the bookings as if they were school choirs or stand-up comedy. Would they have so readily booked concerts glorifying the lives of Stalin or Mussolini or Pol Pot or modern history's other brutal dictators? Australia has long boasted of being close to China, but this is just one indication that if there is closeness it has come without any real comprehension.

So who would stage such events? Two groups calling themselves cultural associations which are, according to Feng, "organisations of the United Front." Feng says that there are at least 300 United Front associations in Sydney alone, and hundreds more in other Australian cities. They can take the form of community groups, "patriotic" associations, business chambers, student associations or hometown groups. The Australian Council for the Promotion of Peaceful Reunification of China is a prominent one. Others include the Chinese Students and Scholars Associations on university campuses, the China–Australia Entrepreneurs Association and the Australian Guangdong Chamber of Commerce.

Christina Wang, the chief executive of the International Cultural Exchange Association, which made the bookings, denied any links with the Chinese government and said all key organisers had been in Australia for decades. "We are artists, we just want to put on a good display of song and dance," she said.

The Mao concerts illuminated the deep schism in the Australian Chinese communities between a pro-Beijing group and a pro-Australian group. "A divide has emerged broadly between two camps: naturalised Australians who migrated in the 1980s and '90s with the spectre of the Tiananmen Square crackdown of 1989 fresh in their memories, and more recent émigrés who have been enriched by China's economic miracle of the past two decades and are emboldened by their country's rise as a major international power," wrote Philip Wen, Beijing correspondent for *The Age* and *The Sydney Morning Herald*.

Feng and friends quickly organised a coalition to object to the Red Songs concerts, the Australian Values Alliance. "We are here to protect our Australian values. We choose to live in this country so we need to protect our home," said spokesman John Hugh. The alliance planned demonstrations outside the two town halls.

The concerts were cancelled amid concern for public safety and poor control of the ticketing system, with many tickets handed out for free. "We don't want there to be a split in the Chinese community," Wang commented. "If this does cause a divide, we are willing to abandon the performances."

With 1.2 million Chinese Australians, or one in twenty of the population, this schism in the community is something Australia probably should understand, at least a little. Professor Feng isn't imagining the hand of the United Front in the Chinese diaspora. It's been hiding in plain view. Indeed, Xi Jinping has called the United Front Work Department one of China's "three magic weapons," together with party-building and armed struggle. He was quoting Mao. Mao described the relationship between the three in 1939, when he was still leading the Communists as a guerilla revolutionary force: "The party is the heroic warrior wielding the two weapons, the united front and the armed struggle, to storm and shatter the enemy's positions."

Xi reinvigorated and enlarged the department after its previous director was arrested in the anti-corruption purge. In 2015, at the annual conference of the United Front Work Department, Xi called on the department to emphasise three new areas of work: overseas Chinese students, representative individuals in new media, and the young generation of entrepreneurs and businessmen. "From the party's Politburo Standing Committee down to its grassroots committees, united front work involves thousands of members, social organisations, and fronts," write two Western experts on the subject, American Peter Mattis and Australian Alex Joske. "Wherever the party is found, be it a government ministry or a party committee in a joint venture, the united front system is likely to be operating." That includes China's embassies and consulates.

Something as minor as the cancellation of the two concerts celebrating Mao was, in fact, an important victory, according to Feng. "I'm very happy about it. This is regarded as the first victory, that a performance of Red culture has been blocked overseas. It's had an impact on Chinese communities around the world."

In 2018, the United Front Work Department was strengthened when work on religious groups, ethnic minorities and the Chinese diaspora was explicitly placed under its control, and it was formally given control of three State Council (cabinet equivalent) agencies responsible for work in those areas: the Overseas Chinese Affairs Office, the State Administration for Religious Affairs, and the State Ethnic Affairs Commission.

In Australia, the United Front Work Department has had much more to work with in recent years. "With mainland Chinese migration sharply increasing in recent years, state-backed political astroturfing has become more pronounced, from pro-Beijing South China Sea demonstrations in Melbourne and Sydney, to mobilising cheering, flag-waving crowds to drown out Free Tibet and Falun Gong demonstrators during President Xi Jinping's visit in 2014," Wen explained. What are the alignments among the 1.2 million Chinese Australians? "My judgment is that [the] anti-Communist[s] are in a very tiny minority, and die-hard Communist supporters are also a tiny minority, and the vast majority are in between, wavering," says Feng, who migrated from China to Australia in 1995.

*

For John Garnaut, it hit him when he was interviewing a Chinese billionaire in a mock castle. Garnaut was the Beijing correspondent for *The Age* and *The Sydney Morning Herald* when he managed to get the first Australian media interview with the elusive Chau Chak Wing.

The billionaire property developer had been given Australian citizenship and his wife and two of his three children lived in Sydney, but he preferred to live in his home base in the thriving southern Chinese city of Guangzhou, just north of Hong Kong. It was here that he built a mansion with a tower of Australian sandstone, nicknamed his "castle." The castle sat atop a hill surrounded by an enormous complex of plush villas and apartments, complete with the estate's own clubs, schools and golf course, all built by Chau, master of all he surveyed. It would emerge years later that ASIO reportedly suspected Chau, like Huang Xiangmo, to be a covert agent of Chinese government influence.

Sitting down to interview him in his mansion, Garnaut wanted to know about Chau's donations to Australian political parties. Chau was a generous political donor. Even then, in 2009, he'd already given $2 million. That made him the biggest overseas-based donor to the Australian political system. Chau's answer to why he'd been so generous was diplomatic: "I am very happy as a citizen to play my role of participant in the democratic process," he said through an interpreter. But Alexander Downer's answer to why Chau might have given $30,000 to his 2007 re-election committee was hilarious: "Perhaps he just found me incredibly interesting and rather amusing."

Chau's political donations paled in comparison to his donations to two universities. He agreed to give $20 million towards a new Frank Gehry–designed building for the business faculty at UTS, famously built in the likeness of a giant crumpled brown paper bag, plus $5 million for a scholarship fund. And another $15 million for the Chau Chak Wing Museum at the University of Sydney. And those donations were nothing compared to the price he paid James Packer in 2015 for his house in Sydney's Vaucluse. Seventy million dollars. Without actually setting foot inside it.

Even more impressive than Chau's access to money is his access to power. When Xi Jinping travelled to Australia as vice premier in 2010 and invested an unusually long time in getting to know the then prime minister, Kevin Rudd, Chau travelled with him. He has been seen travelling with Xi on other occasions since. China has many billionaires, but very few enjoy such intimacy with the president.

It was Chau's treatment of Garnaut that truly impressed the reporter. In writing up the 2009 interview, Garnaut said that Chau had offered to pay airfares and hotel bills for the reporter and his assistant. Offer declined. Chau sent his chauffeur and black Bentley to pick him up from the airport. Offer accepted. Garnaut later said that Chau had given him a gift bag containing three expensive bottles of French wine at the end of the interview. And another three to his assistant. And followed up with another four later, ten altogether. The wine, which they donated to a charity auction, fetched some $7000. It didn't stop there. Chau also offered to host the reporter and his family for a holiday at his resort, according to Garnaut.

For free. Offer declined. And even offered him a reporting job in which he'd be free to write whatever he wanted. Chau owned a number of newspapers in China and Australia. That offer, too, was declined. The offers were so lavish and so insistent, Garnaut decided, that Chau must have been seeking more than just a soft interview. He believed he was being wooed as part of a larger Chau influence-building effort.

When Chau later sued Garnaut for defamation, Garnaut told the court that he felt Chau had been trying to snare him in a "reciprocity trap" as part of a "web of patronage." Chau told the court he didn't recall giving Garnaut wine. The job offer had been a joke. And he couldn't be sure that the John Garnaut in the courtroom before him was the same person who'd interviewed him years earlier. Chau, incidentally, won the defamation case.

But by then Garnaut had quit his reporting job and gone to work for the then prime minister, Malcolm Turnbull. It was a move with consequences well beyond Garnaut's career. Garnaut had decided that Australia had to wake up to the CCP's plans for the country. That it was his mission to assist the awakening. And that he could better help as an official than as a journalist.

*

So, what does the Chinese Communist Party want from Australia?

Duncan Lewis, who was not only Australia's previous ASIO head but also commander of Australia's Special Forces, secretary of the defence department and Australia's inaugural national security adviser, is especially well qualified to answer. "They are trying to place themselves in a position of advantage," he said in an interview shortly after retiring in September 2019. "Espionage and foreign interference is insidious. Its effects might not present for decades and by that time it's too late. You wake up one day and find decisions made in our country that are not in the interests of our country. Not only in politics but also in the community or in business. It takes over, basically, pulling the strings from offshore." Note that, although Lewis was a longtime soldier, traditional military invasion does not feature in his answer. This is the modern way of intelligent statecraft, conquest and control without war.

Another expert comes to the same conclusion from a very different lifetime of experience. Anson Chan, the former chief secretary of Hong Kong, occupied a position of trust unique in history. She was the last head of the Hong Kong civil service under the British and the first under the Chinese. She served four years under each, evidence that both powers trusted her impartiality and professionalism. The career civil servant, nick-named the "Iron Lady of Hong Kong," is now seventy-nine. "I don't think Australians understand the sort of country they're dealing with. Look at the way they are infiltrating, even in Australia," she said during a visit to Melbourne in 2016. "Australia is a very open society, so it wouldn't occur to most people the designs of the one-party state. And it wouldn't have occurred to the people of Hong Kong until we experienced it firsthand. No one should be under any illusions about the objective of the Communist Party leadership – it's long-term, systematic infiltration of social organisa-tions, media and government. By the time China's infiltration of Australia is readily apparent, it will be too late."

Chan stepped out of retirement to support the campaign to keep Hong Kong's autonomy, as promised by Beijing under the Basic Law. As a result, once trusted by Beijing to administer Hong Kong, she is now denounced in party media as "an important pawn for anti-China forces in the West to meddle in Hong Kong affairs."

Paradoxically, perhaps, while China's conduct outwardly seems offen-sive, from within it is designed to be defensive. "The Chinese Communist Party's priority is to pre-empt all perceived threats to state security," says Samantha Hoffman of the Australian Strategic Policy Institute, an expert on China's use of technology for social control, "which means the Party must not only protect its existing power, but also continuously expand its power outward in what feels like an attack to China's targets."

The prominent New Zealand Sinologist Anne-Marie Brady explains why this came about. From the very beginning of the People's Republic in 1949, "influenced by China's recent history and guided by Marxist-Leninism, the Chinese Communist Party stressed the importance of resolving the foreign presence in China, eradicating the harmful, taking what was useful and bringing it under Chinese control." The system for doing this, its "waishi" system for managing the foreign world, "is a defensive tactic to control the threat of the impact of foreign society on the government's political power," says Brady. The system is "part of a cultural crisis, a conflicting inferiority/superiority crisis that Chinese society has faced since its earliest contacts with the technologically superior Western world in the nineteenth century." To the outsider, it appears that today's China is so mighty that it must have outgrown such timorousness. Yet the psychology and the policies of an impoverished and uncertain new republic of seventy years ago remain operative today.

The good news here is that the CCP's intrusions are not intended to be malicious, but that's little consolation because its intrusions are aggressive nonetheless. Further, it means that its quest for perfect protection is both paranoid and never-ending. You cannot reassure a paranoid person that he or she is secure; nor can you reassure a paranoid political party-state that it is safe. Its systems and policies are structured to expand endlessly. Under this mindset, the greater China's reach, the greater its ability to protect itself. So it must not stop reaching.

Xi has told his party that it must brace for a long ideological struggle. Early in his tenure as president he gave an internal party speech, not released until six years later, in which he said that "the eventual demise of capitalism and the ultimate victory of socialism must be a long historical process." He portrayed China as the challenger striving to defeat a stronger, more established West: "We must profoundly understand the self-regulating ability of capitalist society, fully appraise the objective reality of the long-term advantage of Western developed countries in the economic, scientific and military spheres and conscientiously prepare for all aspects of long-term cooperation and struggle between the two social systems." He warned his party that it would not be "a walk in the park."

It was likely to continue long beyond the lifetime of anyone alive today. He quoted the former paramount leader Deng Xiaoping's 1992 insistence that "consolidating and developing China's socialism will take dozens of generations."

Australia and China have got rich together. For Australia, that is quite enough. But China's government wants more. As much power and influence over Australia as it can possibly get, using fair means or foul. But, as these cases show, what Beijing can get is limited not only by China's abilities, but also by Australia's will. In each case where Chinese officials or agents attempted to intrude, they met Australian resistance. And failed. For all its power, China is neither all-powerful nor irresistible. Australia can shape its engagement with Beijing. There has been considerable cooperation between the two countries. But, as Xi warned, there would be aspects of both "long-term cooperation and struggle." To foreign audiences, however, Xi, and all Chinese government officials and spokespeople, only ever mention one half of the equation – the cooperation, never the struggle. The key to Australia's future with China, if it is to retain its sovereign independence and the liberties of its people as well as the comforts of prosperity, is to find a way to manage both.

TWO GENERATIONS, TWO COUNTRIES

Bob Hawke was halfway through the wrenching, decade-long project to transform Australia. There was pain in the process as factory after factory shut down. It was hard for many to see a happy ending. But Hawke never lost sight of the vision splendid. It was to be a great gift to the country, a gift that still gives today.

Hawke described the Australia he came to lead as having "walked down the gentle path to economic mediocrity." With his treasurer, Paul Keating, Hawke stripped away the tariff protection, opened Australia to the world and rejuvenated an exhausted economy. Together with some consolidation by the Howard–Costello governments that followed, it set the country up for the twenty-eight years of unbroken expansion that we are enjoying to this day. It's been the root source of every job, every opportunity and every new government benefit since. It's been called Australia's "Third Golden Age," following the commodities boom to 1890 and the immediate post-war boom.

After five years of tough dislocation, Hawke wanted to reinvigorate the reform program. He hit on the idea of showing the people a vision of the future, to give the project a clearer purpose, an encouragement to persist. And to keep the people voting Labor, naturally. He turned to Ross Garnaut to conjure it. Garnaut was perfect for the purpose. He was a distinguished economics professor at the Australian National University. He had served as Hawke's economic adviser. Hawke had then appointed him ambassador to Beijing at a time of great Chinese reform and opening. Now, in 1988, he commissioned Garnaut to write a report that would "encourage community discussion and debate" on "Australia's place in the region" and how to go about "adapting our country to realise more fully its almost unbounded economic potential."

Ross Garnaut's report was titled *Australia and the Northeast Asian Ascendancy.* It embraced South Korea, Japan and Taiwan, but at the centre of the opportunity sat China. The report was to be released in 1989. Unhappily, that was the year Beijing unleashed its army against the unarmed student protesters in Tiananmen Square. Hawke's tearful speech in response to the massacre is remembered for its raw humanity: "When all those who had not managed to get away were either dead or wounded, foot soldiers went through the square bayonetting or shooting anybody who was still alive," he said, as his voice quavered and caught. "They had orders that nobody in the square be spared. And children and young girls were slaughtered," he said, as tears began coursing down his face. "Thousands have been killed or injured, the victims of a leadership that seems determined to hold onto the reins of power at any cost. At awful human cost." He announced that all Chinese students living in Australia at the time would have their visas extended, and some 42,000 ultimately were granted permanent residency. His emotions were real and his tears authentic, but he was also a hard-headed leader who would not allow sentimentality to interrupt his plans for the nation. He launched Ross Garnaut's report on how Australia could best take advantage of China's coming boom five months after the massacre.

How did Hawke reconcile his repugnance at China's leaders with his decision to pursue intensified relations? "China remains unquestionably one of the key countries in the Asia-Pacific and it is in all our interests that the decade of openness and reform is not lost irretrievably to the Chinese people or to the region." So he portrayed increased trade as a benefit to China's people, as well as to Australia's. And the prime minister hinted that Australia's engagement with China could exert a moral influence: "A very important element of Garnaut's analysis is that we carry into our relations with Northeast Asia many positive and influential assets. These include – I name only a few of the most important – our proud, vigorous and deeply entrenched democratic traditions, our standards of human rights, our multicultural tolerance, our principles of free trade unionism."

Garnaut's report was a major news event at the time and did exactly what Hawke had hoped. Australia internationalised its economy to take advantage of the China boom to follow, and intensified its political relationship for the same reason. The export of Australian values was less successful than the export of Australian iron ore and meat, however. Democracy, human rights, multicultural tolerance and free trade unionism remain dockside, marooned at our ports, with no buyers in Beijing.

Twenty-six years later, another Australian prime minister commissioned another Garnaut to write another report centred on China. But where Bob Hawke asked Ross Garnaut to write about the opportunity presented by China, Malcolm Turnbull assigned John Garnaut to write about the threat. Two generations of the same family, each responding to their country's needs of the day, each of their lives entwined with the restless relationship between the Middle Kingdom and the Great Southern Land. Ross, in his report, had anticipated a time when China would become the strategic equal of the United States. "This was always going to be a hard time, when it becomes clear that China is, or soon will be, the world's largest economy, with great geo-strategic weight," he says today in an interview. "While China's political shape as it became a developed economy has always been uncertain, the Statue of Liberty was unlikely to be amongst the possibilities. There was always going to be systemic competition between a rich China and the US-led West." He could not have anticipated in 1989 that his fifteen-year-old son would be the one commissioned to advise the Australian government on how the country should protect itself from some of Beijing's most pernicious covert efforts to win it over as part of that competition.

When Hawke sent his father to be Australia's ambassador to Beijing, John Garnaut went with him. He was twelve years old. When John had the opportunity to return to Beijing as a foreign correspondent for *The Sydney Morning Herald* and *The Age* in 2007, after two decades away, he was thrilled. He'd been writing about economics in Australia and now was going to be writing about the most exciting economic story in the world. John Garnaut had fond memories of China and great hopes for its future. "I came to China thinking I knew something about the place," he later wrote. He described himself as a "China optimist." The romance slowly wore off as reality set in. "In those days, I had a simple aspiration: to tell Chinese stories through Chinese voices. I thought Western media focused on the negative, ignoring the progress being made." When he came across the story of two cousins who had survived a coalmine collapse in September 2007, "I thought it was just the kind of uplifting adventure story I was seeking." When he delved, he discovered that the Meng cousins had been left for dead by their bosses, knowingly trapped beneath the surface in the collapsed mine. When their colleagues had moved to rescue the pair, the local Communist Party chief had ordered them locked up to prevent a rescue. It turned out that the mine was illegal. Better to let the Mengs die than concede the existence of an unauthorised mine. When the cousins did manage to dig their way out, half-dead, after six days, they were chased out of town. "It proved to be my first lesson in the brutality of power without accountability," John reflected later.

Another revelation came when he was covering the aftermath of an earthquake in Sichuan province in 2008. Stepping through the corpses and destruction of a ruined town, Garnaut came across a survivor, hanging upside down, with his pelvis crushed between two boulders. "He was alive and had the strength to speak. I told him that if he was brave enough to hang on, the rescue team would come for him," he recounted. "That proved to be a lie. On the highway above, battalions of People's Liberation Army soldiers sat in trucks, eating watermelons and occasionally staging mock-rescues for the benefit of the camera teams that were beaming propaganda footage across the country."

And in writing about one farcical scene, John Garnaut conveyed to readers the difficulty of avoiding being compromised by the party. A cadre had handed him a farewell gift of a leather satchel, and when he reached inside he found a red envelope addressed to his youngest son. He tried to hand the cash envelope back in the street outside his hotel, failed, and instead tossed it into his would-be benefactor's Audi. Garnaut then ran into his hotel, pursued by one of the cadre's aides. As the journalist retreated into the hotel lift, the determined donor tossed the red envelope in behind him. "I banged the open button, just in time, and threw it back after him. It skidded Frisbee-style along the marble, directly through his legs. Success! I slumped against the wall of the elevator as it rose to the eighteenth floor. But then I thought of my two other children, and reached back into the bag. Sure enough there were two more red envelopes. When I returned to the ground floor, the Audi was gone. But the original red envelope was still there, its ten crisp $100 bills untouched in the middle of the hotel lobby — a silent, red memento of how much I still had left to learn."

But it was his encounter with Chau Chak Wing that led John Garnaut to investigate the Chinese government's efforts to increase its influence on Australia. The further he looked, the more alarmed he became. On his return to Australia he set aside plans to write a book and went to work for the prime minister.

Chinese government interference in Australia had already come to Malcolm Turnbull's attention. When John Garnaut joined his staff in 2015, Turnbull gave him security clearance to access all the materials he needed across the various agencies of the federal government to lead the writing of a classified report into Chinese influence operations in Australia. While the report remains classified, its contents alarmed the government sufficiently that it produced two new pieces of legislation to counter Chinese covert intrusions: the National Security Legislation Amendment (Espionage and Foreign Interference) Bill 2018 and the Foreign Influence Transparency Scheme Bill 2018. The first broadens the definition of espionage to include attacks on critical infrastructure such as electricity or telecommunications, and interference with Australian democratic rights using violence or intimidation, and increases the penalty for lying in applications for government security clearances. The second requires anyone acting on behalf of a foreign government to put their name on a public register.

Turnbull presented the legislation to the parliament on the afternoon of 7 December 2017. It was the same day that, after a long and tortuous plebiscite, same-sex marriage was legalised by a vote of the parliament. So the foreign interference bills got scant media attention. They would have been a major story on almost any other day. The prime minister told the parliament: "When the director-general of ASIO, Duncan Lewis, says the threat from espionage and foreign interference is 'unprecedented,' then we know that we must act. The director-general is telling us that the threat we face today is greater than when Soviet agents penetrated the federal government during World War II and the early years of the Cold War."

Turnbull issued a warning to Beijing: "If you are acting to further the interests of a foreign state in ways that are clandestine or deceptive then we will shine light upon your actions and, where necessary, we will shut you down. It means that if you use inducements or threats to manipulate a political process or public debate then we will unleash the full force of powerful new laws and defend our values and democratic institutions. And it means that foreign actors who would do us harm are now on notice: we will not tolerate covert, coercive or corrupting behaviour in our country." How do we know this was directed at Beijing? Because of the prime minister's next words: "Media reports have suggested that the Chinese Communist Party has been working to covertly interfere with our media, our universities and even the decisions of elected representatives right here in this building. We take these reports very seriously." He also cited Russia and North Korea, but this was, above all, a China story.

John Garnaut would later write for the American journal *Foreign Affairs*: "Australia is the canary in the coal mine of Chinese Communist Party interference ... Nobody knows what happens when a mid-sized, open, multicultural nation stands its ground against a rising authoritarian superpower that accounts for one in every three of its export dollars."

A few months later, in July 2018, the chief executive of Donald Trump's successful presidential election campaign, Steve Bannon, used the same metaphor. Australia was the "canary in the mineshaft," he said in an interview. "Australia is at the forefront of the geopolitical contest of our time." But Bannon thought that Australia was losing. Chinese investment had bought control of Australia's economy and was in the process of buying control of its political system, he assessed. "Because of Australia's example, it will not happen here in the US," said Bannon. "It will not be allowed to happen. People are woke." Trump had just announced the first tariffs on China's sales to the United States. The trade war had begun three days before Bannon's comments, and he was exultant. "I can't emphasise Friday night enough – it was the day that President Trump stood up for the American worker."

Others applied different metaphors. To the commander of the US Pacific Command, Admiral Harry Harris, Australia was "the tip of the spear" in the West's efforts to fight back against China's encroachments. That was one of the reasons Harris wanted to be appointed US ambassador to Australia. Donald Trump duly named him to the post in early 2018, only to quickly countermand himself and dispatch Harris to serve as US ambassador to South Korea instead. To a Chinese mainland academic, Australia was a pioneer, and not in a good way. Australia had played a "pioneering role in an anti-China campaign," according to Chen Hong, director of Australian studies at East China University during a visit to Australia this year organised by the Chinese embassy. "The two-way exchanges have been going very well until 2017, when Australia launched this attack on China," he said. "If other countries follow suit, that is going to be recognised as extremely unfriendly. I think the responsibility is totally on the Australian side," Chen said. "China always promotes friendship." Despite some improvements under Scott Morrison, Australia–China relations had entered a freeze, "which in Chinese means a very cold period."

Ross Garnaut showed Australia how to open itself to the China opportunity. A generation later, John Garnaut showed Australia how to protect itself against the China threat. Or, at least, one important dimension of it. Was that the Garnauts, father and son, were so different? They weren't running personal projects or freelancing for their own amusement. Each was responding to the needs of the government of the day as prime ministers sought advice on the problems of the time. Was it that Australia had changed so much? Hawke was Labor and Turnbull Liberal, but both their governments were centrist. Both pursued agendas to internationalise

Australia to trade, to investment, to the Asia-Pacific, to the world. Both sought more intense relationships with China. Hawke opened the iron ore trade with China, for instance. Turnbull's government legislated the China–Australia Free Trade Agreement.

It was not that one Garnaut was so profoundly different to the other or that Australia had changed so radically. It was China that had transformed. The scale of its economy, the resources of its government, the ambition of its leaders, the confidence of its officials had surged. There is no better evidence than Xi Jinping's overturning of Deng's strategic maxim. Deng's injunction that China "hide and bide" gave way to Xi's era of "striving to achieve."

Attesting to its peaceful intent, China for decades liked to point out that it had never maintained an overseas military base. Until it opened one in the African nation of Djibouti in 2017. Beijing always insisted that it was a country that respected international law. Until it rode roughshod over its neighbours' claims and built islands and military bases on contested areas of the South China Sea, flagrantly disregarding a finding by the Permanent Court of Arbitration in The Hague that it had "no historical rights." And Beijing still maintains that it does not spy or intrude on Australia. Although ASIO's chief, Duncan Lewis, said in 2018 that foreign interference in Australia was "unprecedented," and in 2019 that it posed an "existential threat" to the state. While at ASIO he was careful not to single out China. But in an interview immediately after retiring, he said that while it was not only China that preoccupied the Australian authorities, it was "overwhelmingly" China.

What had *not* changed was the foundational psychology of the Chinese Communist Party. The party was founded as a covert, guerilla, revolutionary movement. After it succeeded in seizing power, it created the machinery of state and now operates one of the world's greatest powers. But the party's thinking and behaviour is still strongly influenced by the mentality of the covert, guerilla, revolutionary movement founded in 1921.

What does China want from the world? Mao Zedong gave us a pretty strong clue. The founder of modern China issued a 1956 catchphrase, famous in China: "Use the past to serve the present, make the foreign serve China." The Sinologist Anne-Marie Brady has said that this slogan "symbolises the Chinese Communist Party's policy on the suspect past and the corrupting foreign."

Xi has forcefully revived Mao's personality cult, his worldview and his teachings. He has prohibited any criticism of Mao's leadership, even his disastrous Great Leap Forward and shattering Cultural Revolution. And Xi is following the advice contained in Mao's 1956 slogan. Xi is using China's past, its "century of humiliation," to energise popular support for his Dream of the great rejuvenation of the Chinese nation. And Xi is using the foreign to serve China in several ways.

Xi's signature formulation for his plans for the outside world is to create a "community of common destiny," also translated as "community of shared destiny." The destiny in his vision may be common to the region and the world, but the authorship is exclusive to Beijing. There is no suggestion that Bangkok, Tokyo, Manila, Hanoi, Jakarta, Ulaanbaatar, Canberra, Suva or Delhi is to be given a say in the design of this destiny. Yet all are embraced by its designers in Beijing.

Japan's prime minister, Shinzo Abe, is no enthusiast for Xi's "common destiny." He has accused China of being a destabilising force in Asia. He said that relations between Japan and China today were in a "similar situation" to those between Britain and Germany before 1914. Britain and Germany had close ties and went to war against each other nonetheless, he said. Beijing scolded him for this.

Xi simply ignores the reservations of other leaders and presses ahead with his plans. When he propounded the idea of a "community of common destiny" in a speech, it was translated into English and posted on the homepage of the Chinese embassy's website in Canberra. Asked which countries were envisaged to be part of this community, an embassy official replied: "All countries."

This ambition seems preposterous and isn't meant literally, but, for those willing to join, Xi's ambition is supported by the scope and scale of his Belt and Road initiative. According to China's authorities, 115 countries had formally signed up to join Beijing's plan by April 2019. That's most of the countries on the planet. And Xi has called for more to join. Australia is invited too. A sceptical Canberra has temporised politely while it asks China for detail on governance and other matters.

Xi poetically proposed Belt and Road as a twenty-first-century version of the ancient Silk Road, the storied routes trod by traders from Europe selling horses, honey and slaves to the East in exchange for silk, spices and gunpowder. The Silk Road operated from the time China's Han dynasty decided it would trade with the West, 130 years before the birth of Christ, until the Ottoman empire closed it 1500 years later. In between, Marco Polo travelled the Silk Road and brought back to European readers their first glimpse of the wonders and riches of Asia in his *Marvels of the World*. It was indeed a marvellous time for China, then the world's dominant economy. It had built "a centralised, merit-based bureaucracy that was able to register its population, levy uniform taxes, control the military and regulate society some eighteen hundred years before a similar state was to emerge in Europe," Francis Fukuyama notes. Imperial China built the Great Wall and the Great Canal, projects on a scale dazzling to Europeans. So for China to launch a modernised Silk Road redolent of its glories of yesteryear was a clever domestic political stroke by a leader promising the great rejuvenation of the Chinese nation.

It's also good economics. At a time when the US president is calling for an end to globalisation, Xi is opening new channels of economic activity for China and its many partners. And it's shrewd strategy. While the United States is trying to work out how to extract its remaining troops from the never-ending war in Afghanistan, Chinese engineers are laying fibre-optic cable through that country.

Belt and Road is also a strategic initiative. China uses infrastructure as the friendly forerunner of political power. A Chinese military theorist and a general in the People's Liberation Army Air Force, Qiao Liang, described Belt and Road as "truly the strategy of the shrewd." He explained: "If you tell people, 'I come with political and ideological intentions,' who will accept you?" But if one offers to build scores of highways, fast rail networks, ports and power plants, who can resist?

This is not news to the people of Tibet or Xinjiang. The CCP built a road into Tibet and the Tibetans were excited – it was their first highway: "We were promised peace and prosperity with the highway, and our parents and grandparents joined in building the road," as the president of Tibet's government in exile, Lobsang Sangay, tells the story. "In fact, they were paid silver coins to help them build the road. So there was a popular song during those days, it goes like this: Chinese are like our parents; when they come, they shower you with silver coins," the Harvard-educated lawyer recounted at the National Press Club in Canberra in 2017. The Chinese soldiers were patient with the local kids and bore their taunts with smiles, he said. "Then they built the road. Once the road reached Lhasa – the capital city of Tibet – first trucks came, then guns came, then tanks came. Soon, Tibet was occupied. So it started with the road."

The CCP built roads into Xinjiang, the Muslim-majority lands just to the north of Tibet, too. "When the Chinese people first went to Xinjiang, we all thought, what nice people," says the voice of the ethnic Uighur people's independence movement in the region, Rebiya Kadeer. "We treated them nicely, we expected some investment and development. Initially they said, 'We will help you with development, but you will rule over the land,'" says Kadeer, once one of the richest women in China and a member of China's National People's Congress, now living in exile in the United States. "Only 3 per cent of the people in Xinjiang were Chinese," Mandarin-speaking ethnic Han Chinese, distinct from the Turkic-speaking Uighur who make up the biggest ethnic group in what is now a province of China. The Beijing government operates a transmigration policy in Tibet and

Xinjiang, relocating Han people from the south to change the ethnic and political composition. Han Chinese now make up about 40 per cent of the population in Xinjiang. "They increased and increased and now they are killing us," says Kadeer. The CCP has built a network of re-education camps for the Uighurs. Kadeer calls them concentration camps, where people are detained indefinitely without due process.

The cases of Tibet and Xinjiang are ones where China has a historical claim, dating back over centuries, for asserting sovereign ownership. Both involve lands adjoining China's heartland. They are cases of China consolidating power on its periphery. They are not stories of the CCP conquering foreign nation-states. But they are, nonetheless, instructive tales of how Beijing has used attractive infrastructure as the undeclared vanguard of an uglier political dominance.

Chinese lenders had supplied US$440 billion to finance Belt and Road projects by April 2019, according to China's central bank, already three times the US$130 billion cost of the US post-war Marshall Plan that helped rebuild Europe, adjusted to current dollars. The ultimate sum of investment is widely estimated to be at least US$1 trillion, but if the Belt and Road vision is fully built as originally described by Xi, the total cost would be as much as US$8 trillion, estimates China's State Council.

It is already the biggest international infrastructure project since the Roman Empire. Indeed, the home of the Roman Empire, Italy, has signed up to participate. The 115 signatory countries don't include lesser entities, individual provincial governments such as that of the Australian state of Victoria. Daniel Andrews' government signed a formal agreement with Beijing to participate in Belt and Road. The contents remain secret.

While the transport projects have been its most publicised features, Belt and Road encompasses much more. Indeed, in Xi's original exposition of the plan's "five links," he didn't list the infrastructure first but "policy coordination," government-to-government links and dealings to establish agreed protocols and rules. Only after that did Xi rank the other four:

"infrastructure connectivity, unimpeded trade, financial integration and people-to-people communication." It includes a fibre-optic "digital silk road," an "academic silk road" connecting scores of universities across dozens of countries, and an "investment silk road" flowing with tens of billions of dollars' worth of corporate investment already and strewn with Chinese economic cooperation zones. And embedded within it is the "string of pearls," a poetic name for a military project.

The "string of pearls" is an international chain of ports that China is building or leasing to allow it control of the Indian Ocean. The ports in Myanmar, Bangladesh, Sri Lanka, the Maldives and Pakistan reach along the vital maritime trade corridor connecting China to its oil supply in the Middle East. Beijing emphasises that all its port arrangements are strictly commercial. Analysts in India, the United States and elsewhere point out that the ports are dual-use, able to accommodate Chinese warships as well as merchant ships. An anxious India is seeking to counter with its own "chain of flowers."

The idea of Xi's "community of common destiny" derives from an ancient Chinese concept, All-Under-Heaven or *tianxia*. On the basis of this concept, Chinese emperors claimed the Mandate of Heaven to unite all under their rule on earth. Japan created its own version, "Eight Realms Under One Rule,' and adopted it for its World War II campaign of conquest of all Asia and the Pacific – "the Greater East Asia Co-prosperity Sphere." Xi's "community of common destiny," says the Australian Sinologist Geremie Barmé, "provides substance and diplomatic architecture to the revived concept of all-under-heaven or *tianxia*, one which assumes a belief that China can be a moral, political and economic great power." And if you think that such words and concepts are unimportant to the Chinese system, Barmé would remind you of the line from the *Analects* of Confucius: "He who does not understand words is incapable of understanding men." We might also keep in mind that what Westerners call propaganda the CCP calls "thought work." Words and ideas are the essential foundation of every concrete act.

Casting ahead, Barmé suggests that as the theme of a "community of common destiny" becomes "further embedded in Chinese official discourse, and as China more confidently engages in global governance, an abiding element of China's Maoist era — that of the collective outweighing the individual in every sphere of activity — will continue to shape the country's behaviour internally, as well as externally."

The gilded lure of a Chinese-funded "community of common destiny" isn't Beijing's only mechanism for making the foreign serve China. Economic coercion is an important tool of Chinese statecraft. When the Reserve Bank's Philip Lowe cited the "political difference" between Australia and China, he was too diplomatic to speak plainly the central one: China is an authoritarian country. Australia is a democracy. And this introduces a peculiar risk. The Chinese authorities don't think of international business or finance in the same way that people elsewhere do. Whenever an Australian business manager celebrates a breakthrough into the Chinese market, a CCP official notes it as a possible future pressure point. When an Australian government minister proudly announces a new trade opening into China, Beijing counts it as a new source of leverage against the Australian government. Beijing's motto could be summarised as: "Your deal, our leverage." It's an alien concept for most people in democratic systems, where trading is conducted for mutual advantage. That's naive in the worldview of the CCP. The trade will be allowed to proceed to mutual advantage unless and until Beijing needs to take control for sole advantage.

In China, business does not exist in a universe separate to politics. Business, like everything else, is subordinate to politics. Xi has given this new stridency. All Chinese state-owned firms have long had internal party committees to offer "guidance." Now Xi's government requires that all foreign companies in China set up such committees, and all listed Chinese companies too. The party's intrusion into private firms "is not a discrete effort to infiltrate the private sector per se, but rather is a manifestation of the CCP's desire to have insight and input into all economic, civil, and political activity within the country," says Jude Blanchette, China adviser with the US-based geopolitical advisory business Crumpton Group.

When Zhu Rongji proposed that we "all get rich together," he didn't disclose the second half of the formula. Getting rich with China means getting ready to be pressured by China. A pair of China experts tried to warn Australian businesspeople and government officials in 2017. Australia's economic relationship with China has flourished, "but this flourishing relationship also gives ... China the increased ability to threaten and use economic coercion in its relations with Australia," wrote Linda Jakobson and Bates Gill in their book *China Matters: Getting It Right for Australia*. "Australian political leaders and the broader public need to be aware of the pronounced intertwining of security and economic interests with China [and] the ways in which Chinese can exercise economic hard power."

Is this all just a bit paranoid? On the contrary. Nothing could be as ordinary as Beijing using economic coercion against its trading partners. In the past ten years, Beijing has imposed economic punishment on at least eleven countries, for a wide range of perceived offences. This does not include China's trade war with the United States in 2019, where the US was the aggressor and China the respondent. In each of the eleven punishments, Beijing imposed an economic penalty for a non-economic action. They varied in the particular but were consistent in the pattern. The Chinese government went after countries large and small, on several continents, over a range of grievances. The countries punished were, in chronological order, France, Japan, Norway, the Philippines, the UK, Taiwan, Mongolia, South Korea, Palau, Canada and Australia. Typically, the Chinese government found a pretext rather than announcing a reason. Ambiguity is important to Beijing, as we'll see. It generally chose very specific interests to hit, rather than imposing economy-wide sanctions. And while it has not met with 100 per cent success, it has had substantial impact. If China's government is aiming to train the world to fear its wrath, it would seem, by and large, to be succeeding.

A brisk walk through these cases starts with the 2008 decision by French president Nicolas Sarkozy to meet the Dalai Lama, considered a spiritual leader by many Tibetans and a reviled "splittist" pursuing Tibetan independence by the CCP. In response, Beijing suspended a multi-billion-dollar order for 150 Airbus planes and cancelled two big-spending trade missions to France. The link was clear, but never stated openly. China's then premier, Wen Jiabao, leading a major Chinese trade delegation around Europe, winked: "I looked at a map of Europe on the plane. My trip goes around France ... We all know why." Paris recanted within weeks. The flow of deals resumed. Sarkozy's meeting with the Dalai Lama was the last by a French president. Asked last year whether he would meet the spiritual leader of the Tibetan people, President Emmanuel Macron said: "Is it good for my people if I have a sort of counter-measures coming from China" as a result of such a meeting? "For sure, no."

The next case grew out of a Chinese territorial dispute with Japan. Tokyo administers a tiny clutch of islands, known as the Senkakus in Japanese and the Diaoyu in Chinese. Beijing claims sovereignty over the islands, situated in the East China Sea. In maritime jostling in 2010, a Chinese fishing trawler collided with two Japanese coastguard vessels. The Japanese detained the Chinese skipper. Beijing retaliated, while never drawing the connection explicitly. It said that it was cutting exports of rare earths, a group of seventeen metals of strategic importance, to countries including Japan. It so happened that Japan was more acutely affected than others. Rare earths are essential to a wide array of computer and electronic products, from mobile phones to guided missiles. Beijing controlled about 95 per cent of global exports of refined rare earths at the time. While China's government said that it was restricting output for environmental reasons, the World Trade Organization rejected this explanation and ruled against it. Japan decided it needed to protect future access to these strategic metals by sponsoring more developments outside China. This included critical Japanese support for an Australian company, Lynas Corporation, which is today the most important source of refined rare earths outside China. In this way, the episode rebounded on Beijing because Japan took insurance against future coercion. China's grip on the global supply slipped to 85 per cent. But it also worked for China: Japan has not detained any more of its ships' crews. Beijing's official media this year again have threatened to use China's rare earths dominance for coercive purposes. This time against the United States as part of the trade war between the two great economies. Alarmed at the risk, Washington has since started discussions with Canberra over ways to bring more Australian rare earths onto the market to dilute Chinese dominance, much as Japan did after the maritime incident.

The month after the clash with Japan, China acted against Norway, case study number three. The Norwegian Nobel Committee awarded the Peace Prize to Chinese writer and democracy advocate Liu Xiaobo. China froze diplomatic contacts, suspended free trade negotiations and cut imports of Norwegian salmon, supposedly because of "food safety" concerns. The sanctions remained in place for more than three years, until Norway buckled. Its prime minister declined to meet the Dalai Lama, and the foreign minister pledged not to support "any behaviour that harms China's core and important interests."

In the fourth case, that of the Philippines, Manila was punished for standing up to China over a territorial dispute in the South China Sea in 2012. Beijing cut imports of its bananas, supposedly over pests in the fruit. And while bananas may sound a trivial target, they're a serious export for the Philippines and the losses were in the billions of dollars. When President Rodrigo Duterte buckled, visiting Beijing in 2016 and announcing the Philippines' "separation" from its longtime ally, the United States, the banana trade rebounded and Xi Jinping announced US$24 billion in new investments.

In the case of Britain, high-level contact was frozen after Prime Minister David Cameron met the Dalai Lama in 2012. It resumed after Cameron emphasised in the House of Commons that Britain was firmly opposed to Tibetan independence. He told Chinese investors: "We want to be the destination for Chinese investment. Tell the other Chinese investors — come to London; spend your money." Beijing responded by announcing £14 billion in investment in 2014.

When Taiwan's voters ignored Beijing's preference in 2016 and elected as president the candidate for the Democratic Progressive Party, Tsai Ing-wen, in a landslide, China cut its flow of tourists to the island. The number of mainland visitors fell by more than one million a year, a quarter of the total. Beijing imposed a political freeze and other measures, including intensified military exercises. The DPP favours independence from Beijing; its main rival, the Kuomintang, favours unification. Tsai has not resiled from her party's position. In 2019, she has been an outspoken supporter of the Hong Kong protest movement. Beijing, which until now has restricted tour groups, said in July 2019 that it would also curb individual Chinese travelling to Taiwan. Tsai will stand for re-election next year.

Case seven. Mongolia allowed the Dalai Lama to visit in 2016, his third time in a decade. It was one of his predecessors who brought Tibetan Buddhism to Mongolia in the sixteenth century. But neighbouring Beijing buys 90 per cent of the tiny democracy's exports. It punished Mongolia by imposing tariffs on its mining exports and freezing negotiations over loans. The government in Ulaanbataar quickly expressed regret and promised not to repeat the offence. China relaxed its sanctions. In this case, China did not try to conceal the cause and openly cited the Dalai Lama's visit. "We hope that Mongolia has taken this lesson to heart," said its foreign ministry.

In 2017 it was South Korea's turn. When it sought to protect itself from North Korean missile attacks by installing a US-made-and-operated missile defence system, China cut its group tours. Tourism numbers fell by 60 per cent. The cost to South Korea's tourism industry was US$6.8 billion, according to its parliamentary budget office. Beijing also shut down much of the "K-pop" industry's burgeoning sales to China – music, TV and film. The sanctions affected 57 per cent of all South Korean firms, according to a local trade association's survey. The sanctions played directly into South Korea's presidential elections – the opposition candidate took advantage of the situation by promising to cancel the missile defence system's deployment if elected. He is now president and relations are repaired. China insisted throughout that its punishment of Seoul was, in fact, the "voice of the people," a spontaneous Chinese people's consumer movement that had nothing to do with the government.

It was also the year to punish Palau, case nine. Palau is a country so remote and so small that many have never heard of it. This South Pacific micro-state has a population of 20,000. It is a sovereign state in a close relationship – a "Compact of Free Association" – with the United States, which provides its defence and funding for other services. The other key fact about Palau is that it is one of the very few countries to recognise Taiwan, not the People's Republic, as the sole legitimate government of China.

In 2008, there were just 638 Chinese visitors to Palau. China's tourism industry pumped this up to 91,000 by 2015. And then, two years later, Beijing told its tourism operators to shut off group tours to Palau under pain of fines. No explanation was given. The number of Chinese visitors fell to 58,000 in 2017, an abrupt decline of more than a third.

China's campaign to persuade nations to switch recognition from Taiwan to Beijing has intensified. Since Tsai won Taiwan's presidency, seven countries have changed allegiance to Beijing. That includes two South Pacific nations, Solomon Islands and Kiribati. Only fifteen capitals worldwide remain allied to Taiwan. Despite the shattering effect on the Palau economy, its president is standing firm in the face of the so-called "China ban," refusing to switch recognition to Beijing, and seeking economic help from the United States, Japan and South Korea as he prepares to go to the polls in 2020. President Tommy Remengesau Jr said that "friendship is earned, not forced."

Canada was next, number ten. Its crime was to act on an American request to arrest in December 2018 a Chinese business executive accused of committing bank fraud in the United States. Meng Wanzhou worked as chief financial officer for the Chinese telecommunications giant Huawei.

A US request to extradite her to America for trial is before the Canadian courts. Beijing demanded her immediate release and threatened unspecified "serious consequences." Nine days after the Canadians arrested Meng, the Chinese authorities detained two Canadians, former diplomat Michael Kovrig and business consultant Michael Spavor. They remain under arrest, accused of spying in general, without specific charge. Prime Minister Justin Trudeau described the arrests as arbitrary, the men "detained for political reasons." He added: "China is making stronger moves than it has before to try to get its own way on the world stage and Western countries and democracies around the world are pointing out [that] this is not something we need to continue to allow." Beijing inflicted the further punishment of cutting imports of Canadian canola, potentially a US$2 billion loss, and beef and pork, a possible further loss of half a billion US dollars a year. The Chinese government says the food bans are due to food safety issues. The Canadian opposition leader has accused Trudeau of weakness in the face of Chinese bullying and urged him to impose retaliatory trade sanctions on China. It was a contested issue heading into Canada's October election.

Finally, Australia. In February 2019, it became clear that China's authorities had ordered extra checks on Australian thermal coal imports. The news agency Reuters reported that Australia's product was to be subjected to extra "environmental" inspections and clearing time would be extended. Normal processing time of between five and twenty days was to be extended to at least forty days. While China was seeking to reduce its overall imports of coal, imports from Indonesia, Russia and elsewhere were not affected. The Australian dollar lost 1 per cent of its value on the news. Australia's thermal coal exports to China in 2018 earned $4.9 billion in export income, not the biggest item but among the top half-dozen. The Morrison government said it would seek clarification from Beijing. By July more than $1 billion worth of Australian thermal coal, used for generating electricity, was piled up on China's docks awaiting customs clearance, according to industry newsletter *Platts*. "People who are buying Australian coal have switched," Rory Simington, principal analyst at global energy consultancy Wood Mackenzie, told *The Guardian*. "If you have a vessel that is sitting outside a port for three months waiting for clearance you're going to buy Indonesian or Russian coal which isn't going to be delayed." By August the Morrison government was still "seeking clarification" from Beijing. Six months after the Reuters report, trade minister Simon Birmingham said, "We do want to get to the bottom" of the situation and that he was seeking "further dialogue."

Why the go-slow? And why the mystery? "They're looking to send a signal," said Griffith University political science professor Andrew O'Neil. "If I had to put money on it, I would say there was a political and strategic dimension to this decision." The former secretary of the Department of Foreign Affairs and Trade, Peter Varghese, now chancellor of the University of Queensland, concurred: "Personally, I think they probably are trying to signal to Australia." It's a signal of displeasure. Beijing does not like Australia's ban on participation by China's companies, Huawei and ZTE in particular, in building the 5G wifi network. And it doesn't like the Turnbull government's legislation to curb foreign interference in Australia, a law passed with the support of the Labor Party. "Taking countries in and out of the deep freeze is a well-tested Chinese strategy," said Varghese. Confirming that this is exactly what Beijing had done, the director of Australian studies at East China Normal University, Chen Hong, said in September that Australia's relations with China had entered a "freeze." The freeze extended to high-level diplomatic visits.

So why doesn't Beijing just say so? Why not let countries know explicitly that they are being punished, as the United States does when it imposes trade sanctions on other countries? The US announces its displeasure, gives its reasons, and imposes punishment accordingly. Sometimes, especially in the Trump presidency, the official justification is disingenuous. But the transgressor state knows exactly who is hurting it and they have a pretty clear idea why, thanks to the presidential Twitter feed. An offending nation is being hit according to the Trump Doctrine, as put to *The Atlantic*'s Jeffrey

Goldberg by an unnamed White House official: "The Trump Doctrine is 'We're America, Bitch.' That's the Trump Doctrine."

The CCP operates very differently. "You are never going to get clarification from the Chinese system of whether they are signalling something or whether it's a more routine trade matter," Varghese explains.

> It's part of their strategy. They leave it to you to guess. They let you go through the process of thinking, 'What could we have possibly done to upset the Chinese?' They leave us to use our imaginations to think of what we might have done. This is the same principle – the self-criticism – that the party used to pressure suspects during the Cultural Revolution.
>
> Then they wait while you take it to the next step. You identify it yourself. Once you've come to your list of possibilities of what they might be upset about, you try to fix it. There's an element of tactics to it. The whole pattern of Chinese exercise of influence and control is to bring pre-emptive concessions to China so that they don't have invade or do anything so unsubtle.

It is, in other words, a process of conditioning. Beijing uses uncertainty over the reason for punishment to train countries into anticipating its wishes and fearing its wrath. Better than telling other countries how to serve China, Beijing trains them into doing it themselves. Unbidden.

Simon Birmingham will be waiting a long time for formal confirmation from Beijing that the coal go-slow is the result of a political decision to discipline Australia. Varghese again: "You end up so that countries automatically ask themselves the question, 'Is my next step going to annoy the Chinese, and therefore I'd better not do it.'"

Beijing's policy of aggressive ambiguity serves three other purposes. It allows China to pose as a benign power offering only "win-win" outcomes. It protects China from any country that might want to seek formal recourse by taking a case to the World Trade Organization. And it gives uncertain or fearful governments the option of pretending nothing political is going wrong, of playing along with the Chinese fiction to avoid open confrontation. Australia falls into this category, preferring not to talk about the problem.

There are six important features of the policy. First, this is not a policy that Xi Jinping started. The People's Republic of China has used it for decades. But it has been extended to more countries, more aggressively, under Xi. Second, it's being used as an all-purpose punishment. In this sample of eleven cases, it was used to influence other countries' election outcomes, defence options, territorial claims, peace awards, telecommunications decisions, laws against foreign interference, arrests of Chinese citizens wanted abroad, diplomatic recognition of Taiwan and hosting of the Dalai Lama. Third, pain has been applied across a wide variety of economic fields. Beijing has applied it to trade in goods from aircraft to bananas, to services like tourism and music, to infrastructure such as telecommunications, and to investment too. This means that any company or any industry anywhere can be punished for the decisions of a country's national government, or even for the choices of its voters. It is a form of collective punishment. Fourth, China deploys economic pain quite carefully to avoid hurting itself. It targeted Norwegian salmon, for instance, rather than its oil-drilling firms, on which China relies. It chose to hit Australian thermal coal, a commodity in plentiful supply from many suppliers, including domestic Chinese ones, rather than its iron ore, on which China heavily relies. Fifth, a country cannot assume it will be protected by its size or geography. Beijing has struck major powers as well as minnows, in Europe, Asia, the Pacific, North America and Oceania. Only one country has been conspicuously spared: the United States. While France and Britain were punished for hosting the Dalai Lama, the US has hosted him without consequence. Beijing presumably did not want to provoke Washington because of America's size, its readiness to retaliate, and the fact that China's grand, systemic challenge to US power is a much greater priority than the urge to deter Dalai Lama visits or other lesser matters. Finally and most importantly, China's coercion doesn't always work. Sometimes it simply meets resistance. The coal ban certainly didn't change Australian policy. Canada has not yielded to China's tactics – not yet, at least. Even tiny Palau is standing its ground, putting bigger powers like Britain and France to shame. Sometimes China's bullying backfires. The attempt to pressure Japan only made Japan more resilient.

Sydney University's James Reilly said in 2013: "Never in world history has one government had so much control over so much wealth. It is no surprise, therefore, that Beijing is deploying its vast economic wealth to advance foreign policy goals. China is using economic statecraft more frequently, more assertively, and in more diverse fashion than ever before." As he wrote that, Xi was only just unveiling the Belt and Road plan.

Mao could not have imagined a China with so many options – some seductive, some subversive and some coercive – for making the foreign serve China. And all of this without so much as mentioning the People's Liberation Army and its capacity to wage war.

The internet has made so big a change to the nature of warfare that the previous top military officer in the United States, the chairman of the US Joint Chiefs of Staff, Martin Dempsey, described it as an "inflection point." It was so profound that it "eclipses the introduction of nuclear weapons, the introduction of the air domain and the airplane, and the transition from battleship to aircraft carrier."

This 2012 pronouncement is similar to another one by two officers of the Chinese People's Liberation Army. "We can say with certainty that this," referring to information technology, "is the most important revolution in the history of technology. Its revolutionary significance is not merely in that it is a brand-new technology itself, but more in that it is a kind of bonding agent which can lightly penetrate the layers of barriers between technologies and link various technologies which appear to be totally unrelated." This thought led them on to an idea that seems to prefigure using 5G, or fifth-generation, cellular network technology as a weapon of war: "The new concept of weapons will cause ordinary people and military men alike to be greatly astonished at the fact that commonplace things that are close to them can also become weapons with which to engage in war. We believe that some morning people will awake to discover with surprise that quite a few gentle and kind things have begun to have offensive and lethal characteristics."

This was the reason that Australia, first among governments anywhere, decided to ban Huawei, China's flagship telecoms equipment manufacturer, from building its 5G network, much to the chagrin of the Chinese government. It couldn't be trusted in a network which will reach inside everyone's homes, as well as offices and hospitals and factories and universities and water systems and electricity networks, connecting everything in a system that dispenses with the previous design of core and periphery. To penetrate any part of the network is to penetrate every part. As Malcolm Turnbull liked to say in internal government discussions, "The core is no more." So a malicious intruder could, for example, burn your house down by accessing your toaster through its network connection, or kill you by running your driverless car off the road, or by messing with your 5G-enabled pacemaker. These examples of "gentle and kind things" taking on lethal powers have been used commonly to illustrate one of the risks of the so-called "internet of things." And a malicious hacker could do such things from anywhere, near or far, undetected, and "lightly penetrate the layers of barriers between technologies and link various technologies which appear to be totally unrelated."

The main difference between Dempsey's famous 2012 pronouncement and the thoughts of colonels Qiao Liang and Wang Xiangsui is that the Chinese officers published theirs in a book in 1999, the same year that US researchers first conceived the term "internet of things" after connecting a Coca-Cola vending machine to an internet cable. The fact that the PLA Literature and Arts Publishing House issued the book means that not only was their concept in circulation in Beijing thirteen years before Dempsey's statement, but it also enjoyed the support of at least some elements of the Chinese military leadership. Their book has since been published in multiple editions in English under the title *Unrestricted Warfare*. This is taken from a remark by one of the authors that "the first rule of unrestricted warfare is that there are no rules, with nothing forbidden." It's become a handbook for China hawks in the US, including some in the Trump administration, who see it as a guide to China's plan for asymmetric war against Washington. Later English editions carried a subtitle: *China's Master Plan to Destroy America*. American analysts have seen in the book an echo of the cunning of the ancient Chinese strategist Sun Tzu: "If one party is at war with another, and the other party does not realise it is at war, the party who knows it's at war almost always has the advantage and usually wins."

Qiao and Wang argued that while the Americans were limited by an infatuation with the latest expensive high-tech military hardware, the revolution in military affairs was not to be found in traditional weaponry, but in a new concept of what a weapon might be: "As we see it, a single man-made stock-market crash, a single computer virus invasion, or a single rumor or scandal that results in a fluctuation in the enemy country's exchange rates or exposes the leaders of an enemy country on the Internet, all can be included in the ranks of new-concept weapons." Even if there is no bloodshed, it is still war: "Even if some day all the weapons have been made completely humane" they wrote, "there is no way to change the essence of war, which is one of compulsion, and therefore it cannot alter its cruel outcome, either."

The Chinese are not alone in conceiving of asymmetric war against the United States. If your adversary has the biggest collection of military firepower on earth, a smart warrior doesn't come up with ways to confront it, drawing its fire for certain defeat. A smart warrior thinks of ways to circumvent it. Osama bin Laden didn't attack the Pentagon with guns but with flying lessons for his men and the hijackings of civilian airliners. The Russians didn't risk US intervention in their invasion of Ukraine by flying Sukhoi bombing runs against Kiev and marching infantry columns across the border. They used cyberwar to shut down parts of the Ukrainian electricity grid. On 23 December 2015, the computer systems that control Ukraine's electricity system were taken over by unseen agents. The power plant operators sat helplessly as "ghostly hands moved cursors across their computer screens, opening circuit breakers at fifty substations and shutting off electricity to about 700,000 people." Putin sent so-called "green men" in unmarked fatigues, former Russian soldiers or Russian soldiers on leave, to invade. Invasion? asks Putin. What invasion? In fact, Russia was the first state in history to use a cyber-attack to "soften up" an enemy in preparation for a conventional military strike. That was in the prelude to its invasion of Georgia in 2008. Four years before Martin Dempsey's remarks.

But by far Putin's greatest victory with cyberwar was his calculated interference in the 2016 US presidential election. Russia sowed confusion, mistrust and division that roils the US leadership and political system to this day. It destabilised its principal adversary more effectively than any military strike could have; where a physical attack would have unified the

United States against a foreign enemy, cyberwar has turned it against itself. Notably, the Russians don't use the term "cyberwar." They call it "hybrid war," the merging of conventional and unconventional methods to subdue an enemy.

China is building aircraft carriers, but it isn't relying on them in any clash with the US. Because its inferior force would lose. Not just today. It would take China many years to match the United States in carrier-based warfare. Beijing, thinking asymmetrically, fast-tracked the development of long-range hypersonic missiles, the DF-20 and DF-21, the so-called "carrier killer" missiles. Armed with these, China doesn't need its own fleet of aircraft carriers to force America's carrier battle groups far from the Chinese coastline. US carriers would need to stand offshore at least 1000 nautical miles from China, according to US analysts, in the event of a crisis, to stay beyond China's range. That's new. The missiles do the job much more cheaply and effectively than Chinese carriers could. The US so far has no effective countermeasure.

And, of course, China has put great effort into its offensive cyber capacity. A senior US official used a telling metaphor earlier this year. The National Security Agency's cybersecurity adviser and a former White House cybersecurity coordinator, Rob Joyce, told reporters: "I kind of look at Russia as the hurricane. It comes in fast and hard." China, on the other hand, "is climate change: long, slow, pervasive." Russia strikes for particular disruptive advantage. China wants to take overall advantage of the entire system. And it's winning, according to the consensus of US agencies, as summarised by The Washington Post in March: "China's eating our lunch in cyberspace."

China spends much less on its military. While the United States spent US$649 billion in 2018, China, number two in the world, spent US$250 billion, according to the Stockholm International Peace Research Institute. It was the first time in nine years that US spending had risen. China's has risen annually for twenty-four years now, according to the institute, holding steady at 1.9 per cent of GDP, the same as Australia's ratio, compared to America's 3.2 per cent. The two great powers have different missions, with the United States the only truly global military power, while China's emphasis is the Indo-Pacific region. For now, Beijing isn't seeking to out-match the US, but to outsmart it in its priority region.

According to war games conducted by the US RAND Corporation, the US would lose a war where it fights China and Russia. "In our games, when we fight Russia and China," RAND analyst David Ochmanek said in March, "blue gets its ass handed to it." "In other words, in RAND's wargames," summarised a reporter for the US site *Breaking Defence*, Sydney Freedberg, "the US forces – colored blue on wargame maps – suffer heavy losses in one scenario after another and still can't stop Russia or China – red – from achieving their objectives, like overrunning US allies." In the simulations, the United States is capable of defending its own territory but not others' against a Russian and Chinese attack. RAND is not a fringe group of publicity-seekers, but a think-tank often commissioned by the Pentagon for research projects.

The two stand-out features of China's military strategy are, first, its ability to connect capabilities, and second, its emphasis on asymmetry in defeating an enemy. Knowing the history of the CCP as a covert, guerilla, revolutionary force, which successfully permeates all elements of society at home, and abroad where it can, these strategic strengths are no surprise. In the introduction to *Unrestricted Warfare*, its American publisher William Birnes describes the strategy as one of "waging a war on an adversary with methods so covert at first and seemingly so benign that the party being attacked does not realize it's being attacked." This is merely a military analogue to Beijing's political strategy.

The essential lessons for Australia today? First, this is not an argument to break the US alliance. Australia needs every asset it possesses. It has only one alliance with a great power. It would be reckless to throw this away. The alliance is a force multiplier for Australia. If Canberra were to junk it, Australia would have to spend at least twice as much, 4 per cent of GDP, to recreate the essential benefits that it now enjoys from the alliance, according to Peter Jennings of the Australian Strategic Policy Institute and former chief strategist for the defence department. Neither Beijing nor anyone else is offering to replace the benefits of the US alliance for Australia. But it is an argument that Australia cannot rely on the United States for its security. Through long custom and wishful thinking, Australia clings to the vision of the US as its mighty and ever-dependable saviour. But today, Australia has to accept that this is an imaginary America.

One big change has been in the United States itself. Any pretence of an American security guarantee has been stripped of credibility by a newly erratic president. It's not just the fact that Donald Trump routinely treats America's friends poorly that makes the United States a less reliable ally. That could be a passing phase, as any presidency is. It's the fact that American alliances have become politicised. This takes them into a new realm. The standing and even the existence of US alliances became an issue in US politics at the 2016 presidential elections for the first time since World War II. The Democrat candidate staunchly defended the status quo; the Republican candidate promised a new policy of conditional support for America's alliances. Once elected, Donald Trump followed through on this. His rough handling of US allies has won solid support among Republican voters, but not Democratic ones, illustrating that this has become a polarising political issue.

Another feature of Trump is his reluctance to use military force. He campaigned to end America's agonisingly long wars in Afghanistan and Iraq and bring an exhausted military home. His defence secretary, James Mattis, resigned when Trump sought to continue this policy in Syria, prematurely in Mattis's judgment. Trump pulled US troops out of north-western Syria ten months later regardless, stepping aside so that Turkey could attack. Trump did order the flinging of some fistfuls of missiles at a Syrian air base early in his presidency. This was sporadic and ineffectual and no measure of his preparedness to use force to defend US allies.

If the chances of an American intervention to protect Australia in a crisis previously resembled those of a game of two-up, they are now more like those of the roulette wheel. Would you accept those odds on the preservation of your country?

The other big change is the rise in Chinese capability and ambition. In its chosen theatre of the Asia-Pacific, China is now a peer competitor of the United States. This is new. Even if it were to directly engage China in war, there is no longer any certainty that the US would prevail.

The choice for Australia is not the one we're always being told we have to make — between America and China. It's the choice between the status quo, a wilful complacency, on the one hand. And, on the other, taking action to preserve our liberties from Chinese intrusion and American unreliability.

It was a sunny day in a Melbourne summer, perfect for lunch outdoors. John Garnaut and his wife, Tara Wilkinson, were in the city, without their kids for a bit, and spontaneously decided to eat at one of the restaurants in the city's famous Federation Square. John had left government service with the satisfaction of having seen the parliament act on his classified report into covert Chinese government interference, passing two new laws against it, and now worked as a consultant. But when they sat down at a table at the Chocolate Buddha, the couple found they couldn't enjoy their lunch. Four people approached, separately, and hovered nearby, uncomfortably close. Men and women. They were conspicuous; it was not a very busy time at the Chocolate Buddha. They said nothing, but would stare at John and Tara until the couple turned to look at them, and then quickly look away. One even sat at the same table, but without ordering, until the waiter asked him to move. He then sat at the nearest corner of the next table. It was unnerving, a deliberate act of intimidation.

"How are you?" John asked one woman in Mandarin. She said nothing and abruptly left. But, oddly, she returned ten minutes later wearing a different-coloured shirt. The group persisted even after John and Tara got up to leave, until Tara started to film them with her phone camera. One man was walking directly towards her until she produced the phone, at which he immediately started walking sideways, crab-style, to avoid having his face recorded.

It wasn't the only act of harassment against Garnaut and his family, but it was a notably overt one. The message was plain: you have displeased the Chinese government and we are going to punish you. We can always find you, we know where you live, we can act with impunity in the middle of Australia's biggest cities. We don't care that you worked for a prime minister. We are not afraid of Australia's authorities. It was 24 January 2019. The foreign influence laws had taken effect six weeks earlier.

Their conduct didn't mark them as professionals. But whoever tipped them off to Garnaut's whereabouts probably was. Federal agencies were vexed about how to respond. John and Tara took their problem to Victoria Police. The couple sat down with three plainclothes investigators from the Organised Crime Unit at a café in Little Bourke Street in August. As Tara recounted some of her experiences, one of the police officers leaned forward and interrupted: "Do you realise the people behind you are filming us?" The stalkers helpfully had provided firsthand evidence to the police. An investigation into potential criminal stalking was underway at the time of writing.

The never-ending pursuit of power, the relentlessly expanding influence and the paranoid nature of the Chinese Communist Party means that it will continue to press outwards unless and until it meets resistance. At home and abroad, it imposes one control after another until it is satisfied that it has total control. It is an ideology of authoritarianism animated by a psychology of totalitarianism.

The passage of Australia's foreign interference laws did make a difference. Apart from incurring Beijing's displeasure and earning Australia a place in the Chinese government "freezer," with a ban on high-level visits and a go-slow on Australian coal purchases, that is. The laws did tamp down some of the activity by United Front groups and sobered some of the non-Chinese Australians who, in Soviet times, might have been called "useful idiots" of the Chinese government. Some of the United Front community and cultural associations have become more circumspect about their connections to the Chinese government, removing references from their websites. They have become more cautious in the bellicosity of their statements of support for Chinese government policies. One of the larger United Front affiliates, the Australian Council for the Promotion of Peaceful Reunification of China, has become less active, as it's seized by an internal split over just how overtly pro-Beijing it should be.

Perhaps the most prominent of the pro-China "useful idiots," former foreign affairs minister Bob Carr, has recently left the Australia–China

Relations Institute, which was set up at UTS with a $1.8-million gift from billionaire Huang Xiangmo, a man ASIO found to be a covert agent of Chinese government influence.

Huang was Senator Sam Dastyari's benefactor. Huang personally recruited Carr for the post. Carr said the institute presented "a positive and optimistic" view of Australia's relationship with China. Carr remains at UTS, now as an authority on climate change. The Foreign Influence Transparency Scheme requires that anyone doing the work of a foreign state must put their name on a public register.

The public scrutiny of the purported affiliations of a new federal Liberal MP, Gladys Liu, also shows a new level of intensity. The media and the Opposition demanded to know about the various Chinese community associations listing her as a patron or member. She disavowed them, saying she wasn't aware that they'd claimed her support. As uncomfortable as this was for Liu, it was an illustration of the heightened vigilance about potential covert foreign interference in Australian politics. Liu's extraordinary success as a fundraiser – over $1 million, by her own account, before she'd even been elected to parliament – remains to be probed.

Scott Morrison, in a desperate effort to protect his new MP, accused the opposition of racism. This is a favoured tactic of Beijing. Any scrutiny of Chinese activity is "racist." Morrison should have resisted the urge to do Beijing's work for it.

Australia's former race discrimination commissioner Tim Soutphommasane didn't think it was racist to scrutinise Gladys Liu. "Questioning by Labor and the crossbench members of Parliament on this is legitimate and reasonable," he said.

At the same time, the NSW Independent Commission Against Corruption inquired into NSW Labor MP Ernest Wong, discovering very uncomfortable allegations that he broke the law to conceal illegal donations from Huang Xiangmo. Morrison did not accuse the ICAC of racism in pursuing a Labor MP. The prime minister was wrong to put the exigency of a partisan urge to protect his MP ahead of the higher need to protect his country.

"With these new laws, a democratic pushback has started," says Professor Feng Chongyi. "It starts to change the incentive structure in Australian society, and in particular in the Chinese community in Australia." How so?

> Before, Communist patriots were taking benefit from both sides. They engaged with the United Front to carry out political tasks, and they not only reaped benefit from the Chinese government from doing that, they could also continue reaping benefit from Australian society and Australian government.
>
> Simply because they are backed by Chinese authorities, and by extension the Chinese community, they develop great capacity for fundraising and can raise tens of thousands of dollars at lunches and dinners. Their enhanced ability to raise funds then makes them valued by Australian political parties. They command a lot of followers. They then enjoy high profiles and they enjoy the privilege of meeting leaders in Australian politics, on both sides.
>
> The majority of Chinese Australians have been wavering politically. They want to carry on their normal lives in Australia, but in the meantime they are very, very nationalistic. They are Australian citizens but they have never shown that to the Australian public. But hundreds of thousands of them will come out to wave the red flag to welcome Chinese government visitors.

Modern Australian multiculturalism has no difficulty with the international attachments of immigrants. A Hawke government immigration minister, Robert Ray, liked to quip with various ethnic communities that while he fully expected the first-generation immigrants to cheer for the sports teams from their country of origin, their Australian-born kids should be screaming for the Aussie teams. In other words, we understand that you have ties of sentiment and bonds of kinship to other countries, and we're unconcerned. We know it takes time to put down roots in new social soil. This is a part of democratic pluralism and it's an enrichment of a society. But the nation cannot tolerate acts to advance a foreign political movement with hostile intentions.

The new laws have also helped increase scrutiny of the Confucius Institutes in Australia. Australia's ready embrace of these language and cultural institutions, funded by the Chinese government, is another case of Australia thinking itself close to China when in fact it's been simply uncomprehending. The NSW education department commissioned an independent review of its thirteen Confucius Classroom agreements. It found that "this arrangement places Chinese government appointees inside a NSW government department," and thus that the program had "appointees of a one-party state that exercises censorship in its own country working in a government department in a democratic system." The NSW government is shutting down the scheme. It intends to continue the Chinese learning programs but fund them itself. The thirteen Australian universities that host Confucius Institutes have started to re-examine their arrangements. Four turn out to have given Beijing explicit power to control "teaching quality." This is a surrender of academic freedom in return for foreign government funding.

Probably the single most important act of deterrence was the federal government's decision to reject Huang's application for citizenship and cancel his permanent residency on character grounds. The Australian Tax Office is now pursuing him for $140 million in unpaid taxes. He was at the centre of an important covert influence network. After he bought his $12.8-million Mosman property, local real estate agents were surprised by a flurry of other Chinese buyers asking for similar properties nearby, "and their houses, as we understood it, couldn't be higher than his on the hillside or better than his," a mark of deference to the "King of the Mountain." The particular locale, Beauty Point, was renamed "Beijing Point" by local wags.

But two big questions remain. What about the other suspected covert agents of Chinese government influence working in Australia? Huang was only one of the two Chinese Australian billionaires that ASIO reportedly suspected of being agents of influence. The other, Chau Chak Wing, remains in Australia. And why are the foreign influence laws not being enforced?

The public register, maintained by the attorney-general's department, is a desultory affair. The presidents, patrons, directors and donors of foreign citizenship associations need to put their names on the register if they are representing a foreign government. That's all they need to do – operate openly. There are no costs, no penalties, no stigma. One official likened it to a customs declaration form. At the time of writing, the register contained a scant 181 entries. Most are known, reputable firms and individuals; lobbying businesses; a few foreign companies; only one former Australian minister, Brendan Nelson, who sits on the advisory board of a French firm; and one former official. What about the thousands of other companies and agencies and the tens of thousands of individuals who should register? What about the Confucius Institutes, for instance? People or entities suspected of doing the work of a foreign power are supposed to be issued a "show cause" notice to explain why they haven't registered. Failure to register is a crime punishable by up to five years' jail. None had been issued at the time of writing. If they are found to be representing a foreign power covertly, they should be prosecuted and penalised according to the law, and jailed as the law provides, for up to five years, in serious cases of subversion and espionage. Will this cause diplomatic ructions? Almost certainly. That is not an argument for inaction.

The best defence for the apparent neglect is that the law took effect recently, in December 2018. But if an Australian prime minister announces in parliament that "we will unleash the full force of powerful new laws and defend our values and democratic institutions," and then nothing happens, why would any foreign government take it seriously?

One official said that the enforcement budget was inadequate, and for the same reason ASIO has had to concede publicly that it is being "overwhelmed" by the sheer number of foreign espionage and influence activities underway against Australia. Another said that the government was in consultations to clarify details. The act has already been amended several times for clarity. A third said that the problems of enforcing the scheme were being "sorted out." A fourth stated that the government was too busy "chasing terrorists around the desert in Syria," an important activity but not one that excuses allowing foreign government agents to run amok in Australia. Remember that ASIO chief Duncan Lewis has described terrorism as a serious problem but foreign government interference as an "existential threat" to the Australian state.

Australia has many fine laws that are being flouted through lack of political will. As we've learnt in the last few years, major businesses and famous chefs for years have been systematically underpaying their workers and getting away with it because the Fair Work Commission wasn't enforcing the law. Misconduct by the major banks was rampant because federal agencies lack the staff and the will to investigate. Newly built apartment blocks are uninhabitable because state governments have failed to enforce their building codes.

It is a characteristic of Australia today that governments, state and federal, are failing as functional entities. They have allowed vital laws to lapse through inexcusable neglect. They snap into action only when the media expose a vacuum where there is supposed to be an operational core.

The state, as an entity charged with conducting the rule of law, has been hollowed out. The people live under the assumption that their taxes, their elected representatives and their public servants are protecting them as the law guarantees. But in industry after industry, this has been exposed as a hoax.

Professor Feng is puzzled by the lack of enforcement of the new laws. "In Chinatown, in the Chinese community, there are lots of guys who behave like Huang Xiangmo. Backed by the Chinese authorities, enjoying the support of the Chinese community by extension, they develop great fundraising capacity and become highly valued by Australian political parties. They should be required to explain their activities too." And, as the scandals that continue to spill out of NSW and Victorian state politics demonstrate, there are also quite a few people circulating in state Labor parties who need to explain what they were doing.

It is worse than pointless for parliaments to pass fine laws, for politicians to make grand speeches, if the laws are not enforced. The foreign interference laws, themselves partly the result of a media exposé by the Fairfax newspapers in conjunction with the ABC, appear to be in danger of falling prey to exactly this national lacuna. The four people stalking John and Tara in Melbourne, and whoever had tasked them with their assignment, seemed to think so.

Grand history is on the move and taking a reluctant Australia with it, but at least it's had the decency to offer us a chance to pack a few things first.

The comfortable set-up where an undemanding China supplied ready growth while a benign America kept the world safe for democracy is gone. Australia now needs to work harder for its growth and get active to protect its democracy. Otherwise both are in danger. The world has now entered a low-growth economic reality in a democratic recession. The vital global goods that have sustained our prosperity and our liberty are in dwindling supply. Beijing wants greater control over our country as the price of its business. America's president flirts with dictators, disdains democracies and tests the resilience of the democratic norms of his own country.

But before we are forced out of our comfortable armchair in the first-class lounge of history, we have a moment of respite to design our response to this set of shocks. Xi Jinping's China Dream has hit some unsettling interruptions. Xi suddenly finds himself confronting multiple, urgent problems. He has a pork supply crisis across China, a political crisis in Hong Kong, a foreign policy and trade crisis with America and, overshadowing everything, an economic slowdown. China's private sector, its growth dynamo, shrank last year for the first time in two decades. Many powerful people in China, their interests damaged by Xi's anti-corruption purge, are looking for an opportunity to hurt him. The foreign-policy analyst Allan Gyngell reminds us: "The Chinese political system may be authoritarian, but individuals, institutions and interest groups contend within it."

Xi's moment of distraction is Australia's chance for reflection. Australia cannot live with a China relentlessly pressuring it into submission. But it also cannot live without a solid working relationship with China, including a sound economic relationship.

Beijing is unsure of Australia's position at the moment and is keeping it in the freezer while it decides. "I think it's all in the balance," says Kevin

Rudd, president of the US-based Asia Society Policy Institute. "I think they're waiting to see what the Morrison government is like." Will Australia keep trying to protect itself against China's intrusions? Or will it propose working together? Here's a thought. Let's do both.

At the moment, Australia's China strategy looks like simple status quo, but is actually one of paralysis. Canberra is immobilised by two conflicting policy impulses: the security agencies urge taking a harder line, while the economic and foreign affairs agencies advise against jeopardising Australia's trade with China by doing so. What to do? Australia needs to toughen its protections against China's domineering ways and engage confidently with it for maximum benefit for Australia's people. It needs an energetic engagement, but an armour-plated one, metaphorically speaking.

Some toughening has begun. Much more remains to be done across the full landscape of Australia's society, governance and economy. In confronting these decisions, Australia should not be tremulous, self-censoring or self-limiting, and ought not to live in fear of Beijing's displeasure. Australia often sees itself through the lens of its vulnerabilities to China, and they are real, but it also needs to remember its strengths.

The principal one is mindset, a determination to be proudly ourselves, a distinctive country with our own values and views, our own potential and our own priorities, our own history and our own future, neither Chinese nor American. No country is perfect and Australia has much work to do, but it has achieved for its people the best living conditions available on planet Earth. It ranks consistently in the top two or three, with Norway and Switzerland, in the United Nations' broad measure of living standards, the Human Development Index. Australia has vaulted ahead of both its great and powerful friends of the last two centuries, Britain and the United States, in quality of life. And in the overall level of freedom for its people, too, according to Freedom House.

Many of the richest Chinese, who can command every luxury and privilege at home, nonetheless prefer to live in Australia. "If the relationship between Canberra and Beijing has seen better days, China's ultra-rich appear to be as enamoured with Australia as ever," *The South China Morning Post* reported in 2018. We are the number one choice for rich Chinese looking to migrate, ahead of the United States, Canada and Switzerland. Indeed, the country with the world's biggest outflow of rich migrants is China, and the country with the biggest inflow is Australia, according to the AfrAsia Bank Global Wealth Migration Review 2019. This is a more telling indicator than any amount of nationalist chest-puffing and official propaganda.

For decades, Australia was too ready to concede that Beijing was probably justified in any angry squall over Canberra's behaviour. Most of the time, any hint of Chinese displeasure was reported in much of the media as a righteous reaction and reported uncritically as "China is angry at Australia," rather than realistically as "China is seeking to pressure Australia." If a prime minister hadn't visited Beijing for a while, it was enough to set off a media panic. This condition of national kowtow reached the point of hysteria in 2018 when a former Australian ambassador to Beijing demanded that the foreign affairs minister at the time, Julie Bishop, be sacked. China had stepped up its militarisation of artificial islands in the South China Sea. Bishop had criticised this as destabilising. Beijing said it was unimpressed and continued a two-year freeze on Bishop's visits. Geoff Raby, who'd turned himself into a Beijing-based business consultant, wanted Bishop's head to appease the Chinese government. Prime Minister Turnbull dismissed this nonsense. After the supine Carr as foreign affairs minister, Australia under Bishop had found some spine. Trade continued to boom throughout.

Australia is well on the way to extracting itself from that state of self-imposed servility, at the official level and also, vitally, among the Australian people. When Morrison returned from visiting Washington in September 2019, he was asked whether he was hoping to visit Beijing soon. There had been a three-year hiatus in Australian prime ministerial trips. Morrison refused to play the anxious supplicant: "I'm not waiting by the phone." He was the treasurer who announced the ban on Huawei in Australia's

5G network, and a member of the cabinet that decided to impose the anti-interference laws. Now, as prime minister, he knows better than just about anybody what China's government is seeking to do in Australia, how it blends offers of friendship with efforts at coercion. He shouldn't gush, and he isn't.

But Morrison doesn't like to talk about the problems: "While we will be clear-eyed that our political differences will affect aspects of our engagement, we are determined that our relationship not be dominated by areas of disagreement," he said in his first speech on foreign policy as prime minister. He said he was prepared to make "hard calls" in the national interest, "but they are designed always to leave large scope for cooperation on common interests and recognise the importance of China's economic success. This success is good for China, it is good for Australia." This is an intelligent formula, and a realistic one, but more is required – more hard calls and more cooperation. Many difficult decisions lie ahead: investment approvals; responses to further Chinese government moves in the South China Sea; how to respond to the Belt and Road; how to react to the unfolding events in Hong Kong.

The Australian people also have arrived at a more sceptical view of Beijing's conduct and intentions. The change has been sudden and savage, as measured in the annual Lowy Institute poll of Australians' attitudes to the world. In fact, the chill in feelings towards China was the most dramatic fall in any of the findings in fifteen years of Lowy polling. In 2018, most Australians expressed trust in China. No more. The percentage trusting China fell from 52 to 32 per cent in the 2019 poll. Why the abrupt change? "An important factor in this cooling towards China may be the continuing debate about foreign influence and China's alleged interference in Australian politics," said Lowy's Natasha Kassam. "In 2018, that debate appeared to have gained little traction in the broader population. However, almost half (49 per cent) in 2019 say that foreign interference in Australian politics is 'a critical threat' to Australia's vital interests, an increase of eight points from last year." Beijing has lost the Australian public's support for Belt and

Road, too. Eight in ten people said that it was part of China's plan for regional domination.

Strikingly, Australians want their government to take steps to protect the country from Chinese government threats, military and economic. Even if it's going to come at a cost. More than three-quarters said that the government should do more to restrict China's military activities in the region even if this damages the economic relationship. And while most considered China to be the world's leading economic power, three-quarters of those polled nonetheless thought Australia to be over-dependent on China economically. In other words, the people are in the mood for a toughening of defences against Beijing's coercion. Have we fallen prey to some sort of local Sinophobic hysteria? On the contrary, even after this sharp adjustment, Australians still view China more kindly than do the citizens of many other democracies. A comparative poll of forty-one countries by Pew Research in September 2019 found that the publics in South Korea, Japan, the United States, Canada, Sweden, France and the Netherlands have darker views of China than Australia's public does. Australian opinion towards China turns out to be precisely the median among the countries of the Asia-Pacific and among the countries of Western Europe. Australia's people, on this evidence, are neither rabid nor romantic about China. Just realistic.

With Xi preoccupied with immediate crises, and Australia's people seeking greater protections, the time is ripe for a broad national reappraisal.

Democracy

Democracy isn't just an electoral system to allow the bloodless removal of a bad government, as philosopher Karl Popper described its greatest virtue. Nor is it just a functional embodiment of the sovereignty of the people. It's also a source of national resilience. No democratic government welcomes an economic recession, but we know that Australia will still be a unified nation and a democracy after the next one. China's Communist Party worries that it might not survive a downturn. It has long feared that if it loses economic growth, it will lose its legitimacy too: that the party could fall and calamity ensue.

Australia's democracy is a precious asset, yet it's wide open to manipulation. What is the use of all of Australia's defence force personnel and all its ships and planes if the decision-making system has already been taken over by Beijing? If a foreign power were to command the allegiance of enough key members of Australia's federal political system, Australia's sovereignty would already be lost. Invasion becomes redundant, the ADF impotent. And Sun Tzu's famous dictum realised: "The supreme art of war is to subdue the enemy without fighting."

When the chief of the defence force, Angus Campbell, was this year asked to speak about the nature of war in 2025, it was telling that he devoted his entire speech to political warfare. Authoritarian states, he said, "see war in much broader terms" than democratic ones. "Its reach extends from what we would see as 'peace' right through to nuclear war. In other words, it's a constant of life. For these states, the strategic landscape requires a never-ending struggle. It's a struggle that has been maintained throughout history, and it's a struggle that's happening right now" in the grey zones of political warfare, said Campbell. The first phase of such war is conducted in information campaigns and political activity.

The first line of protection, according to the previous ASIO chief, Duncan Lewis, is the community. "We need a more prepared community," he says, "but we have a way to go yet. ASIO can't do it by itself. ASIO is very dependent on the community to be alert, but not paranoid." He says that the help of the community was essential in defeating terrorism in Australia. The Muslim community, in particular, supplied invaluable warnings to the police and to ASIO and was indispensable to public safety. "The Chinese Australian community could and should be as vital in the work against foreign covert influence, including Beijing's United Front and political corruption."

Australian governments, federal, state and local, as well as schools, universities and community groups, could do much more to educate immigrants and the wider community alike on the value of democracy and the responsibilities of citizens. At the moment the loudest voices of "patriotism" in Australia are the foreign ones manufactured by the covert arms of Beijing's influence operation. There should be a red flag going up here, and not the Chinese national one.

Second are political parties. "I do worry about the issue of financing political parties," says Lewis. "We need a mechanism that maintains parties free of foreign influence." Astonishingly, until 2019 it was legal for foreigners to donate to Australian political parties. The law now forbids foreign donations, but it's still only the barest beginning of fixing Australia's ramshackle political funding system. There have been multiple reports written and recommendations made. Unfortunately, we rely on politicians to make laws to fix the problems of donations to their own parties.

At a minimum, the system needs to be tightened by these steps. One, ban all cash donations; credit cards and bank transfers can be traced, cash cannot. Two, require immediate disclosure of all donations and the identity of the donors on public registers; there is no argument for allowing long reporting lags to remain. Three, impose caps to limit donations to "retail" size of maybe a few thousand dollars or so, rather than permit "wholesale"-sized donors buying outsize influence. Four, enlarge and empower the federal money-tracking agency, AUSTRAC, to enforce the laws and to monitor the sources of funds, to prevent organised crime and foreign sources penetrating the system. Five, create a national integrity commission, or "federal ICAC," to investigate corruption.

Third are MPs and senators. At the moment, there is no systematic scrutiny of politicians to block covert agents of foreign influence from taking seats in parliament. Without due care it can happen and has happened. At the moment, a former intelligence officer for the Chinese government sits in New Zealand's parliament. He didn't disclose this salient fact before running for office. In Australia, Sam Dastyari was operating as an agent for Huang Xiangmo while a sitting senator. There are serious questions about a former member of the NSW parliament, Ernest Wong, now being probed by the NSW ICAC.

Australia relies on chance at the moment: the chance that the media might notice a covert agent of influence; the chance that ASIO might be tipped off; the chance that, if ASIO is tipped off in time, its advice will be heeded. Lewis warned the political parties about Huang, but they continued to accept his money regardless. This haphazard approach must be replaced with a systematic one. All MPs and senators should be required to submit to a formal ASIO security clearance. A reporter put this to Morrison recently as an idea for increasing public confidence in MPs and senators. His reply was that politicians' backgrounds were too diverse. This is an excuse, not a reason. ASIO currently screens thousands of federal public servants and, informally, some politicians too. It should be given the resources and powers to do so formally for all politicians. And if someone running for parliament isn't prepared to submit to a security clearance, they certainly shouldn't be allowed to sit in parliament to make laws.

Fourth is, where possible, bipartisanship. It can be very tempting for an Opposition to make trouble for a government that's struggling to cope with foreign coercion or intrusion. For instance, in Canada the conservatives have been demanding that prime minister Justin Trudeau impose trade sanctions on China in retaliation for Beijing's coercion of Canada. This politicises the issue, undercuts national unity and makes it easier for Beijing to manipulate Canada's political system.

Until now, Australia has been fortunate that the two main parties have been in broad agreement on the need to defeat foreign interference and coercion, and the means for doing so. It's not been perfect – it would have been better had Labor not tolerated Huang's annexing of its NSW branch, for example. And it would have been better had Morrison not labelled legitimate scrutiny of Gladys Liu as racist. But, by and large, the parties have cooperated. One indication: the foreign interference laws passed with bipartisan support. Another: Labor supported the government decision to ban Huawei from the 5G network. A third: when it emerged that

China was waging a go-slow on Australian coal, the Opposition could have chosen to blame Morrison for mismanaging the relationship. It remained silent.

Richard Marles suggests that Australia take bipartisanship on China to another level. Marles, the deputy Labor leader and shadow defence minister, proposes a new structure, perhaps called a strategic council, including relevant members from both main political parties. It would meet and attempt to construct "settled bipartisan positions" on China policy, as Marles puts it, "that almost look like doctrine, so our departments can have confidence of our position not over the next three years but the next thirty years." A strategic council would not be "just some pollies in the members' dining room," he says, but something like a bipartisan cabinet. Its membership would be public, but its proceedings private. It would be properly resourced by the government, with the benefit of full briefings from the public service. "So that we can reconcile the bipolar view that exists in Australia on China – the economic opportunity that China represents, versus the security anxiety that many people feel." Marles says that while the government would have to lead in creating such a mechanism, "I've never felt the need so acutely to get some bipartisanship on this."

Is this undemocratic? Bipartisanship already operates in many areas of Australian policy. The main parties broadly agree on defence, immigration, foreign affairs and intelligence, for example. Marles is proposing a formalisation of the bipartisan approach in one particular area. It would be neither binding nor permanent. It's a good idea, but can the leadership set tribalism aside long enough to do it?

Economy

Australia's economy overall is overexposed to China. That is a vulnerability. Nobody is suggesting that companies turn down profit opportunities. On the contrary. But Australia needs to keep in mind that what we see as an exciting business breakthrough with China can also be used by Beijing as a future pressure point. "Australia calls itself a civilized country, but its behaviour is confusing," wrote *The Global Times*, the most bellicose of Beijing's mouthpieces. "While it is economically dependent on China, it shows little gratitude."

To offset the China risk — whether the risk of Beijing's policy of coercion or the risk of a Chinese economic slump — governments, industries and firms would be wise to take out insurance. China's theatrics so far have been like the Chinese traditional lion dance — all dance, no lion. Yet "sooner or later," says the Lowy Institute's China expert, Richard McGregor, "Australia will be tested. It will be at a time and in a sector of Beijing's choosing. Only then will Australians see if talk about getting tough on China is bluster. How much economic pain can Australia and its politics absorb before we wilt?"

One form of insurance is simply the ancient principle of diversification. This old lesson has been rediscovered by some Australian businesses, which put most of their eggs in the China basket only to find China giving the basket a sudden jolt. The milk companies A2 and Bellamy's, for instance, soared on booming Chinese demand and then were hammered when Beijing abruptly decided to restrict imports to encourage local production. By contrast, diversity saved Australia's thermal coal industry from any serious pain from Beijing's go-slow on Australian imports. While some shipments were caught in Chinese harbours and piled up on docks as Beijing sought to discipline Canberra, most were simply diverted to other markets. "It was real, but it turned out to be a drop in the ocean," according to a leader of one of the major mining houses. The thermal coal market is highly diversified globally. Other industries would have a harder time. Universities come to mind.

Our governments need to work towards diversifying the export markets where Australia sells its wares. To the Morrison government's credit, it is already deep in negotiations to widen trade opportunities with a range of countries. This includes free trade talks with the European Union, and negotiations for a broad Asian regional free trade deal known as RCEP, the Regional Comprehensive Economic Partnership. This is led by the ten

ASEAN nations and embraces China, South Korea, India, Japan, Australia, Indonesia and New Zealand. Both deals are highly prospective, continent-sized opportunities. If the United Kingdom leaves the EU, it will be another, smaller prospect.

The second key type of insurance is the reserve principle, one which no Australian company – or university – is yet applying to its China trade. The chancellor of the University of Queensland, Peter Varghese, thinks they should. Varghese, formerly the secretary of the Department of Foreign Affairs and Trade, last year told a conference of vice-chancellors how the university sector could improve its management of China risk. Instead of spending all the billions in overseas student fees that they collect every year, Australian universities should allocate a percentage of the profit to a long-term investment fund. "So if the tap is turned down sharply, you have a bit more capacity to deal with it," Varghese says. "And you have a bit more for long-term investments like your infrastructure or scholarships or whatever." UQ is now considering just such a fund.

The same principle could be applied to other industries that find themselves overexposed to the whims and wiles of Zhongnanhai, Beijing's red-walled leadership compound. Varghese says that after four decades of effortless profit, the "salad days" of Australia's relationship with China are over. "What lies ahead looks more complicated at best and gloomy at worst," he said in a business speech. "The China of Xi is not the China of Deng, on which most of our China policies have been based." The principle of the resilience fund could be applied by many businesses that find themselves exposed to an export market that carries a high political risk.

Of course, Australia could apply the same principle at the national level. Many countries have sovereign wealth funds, a national buffer against future hardship. Norway's famous US$1 trillion fund, for example, was built from oil profits and designed as a resource for when the oil runs out. The United Arab Emirates has accumulated an even larger sum for the same purpose. Australia has its successful Future Fund, chaired by Peter Costello, to manage some of the surpluses he delivered as treasurer. This is a much smaller fund, designed only to pay for the retirement liabilities of federal public servants, but applies the same principle of basic prudence.

For a country more dependent on trade with China than any other, Australia should consider establishing a similar national resilience fund against the day when China seeks to punish Australia, or the day when China's economy suffers some dislocation. In Aesop's fable of the ant and the grasshopper, the industrious ant works hard and stockpiles food for the coming winter. The complacent grasshopper doesn't see the point. "Why worry about winter?" he asks the busy ant. "We have plenty of food at present." We know what happened when winter came. If the worst should happen, and China decides for political reasons to shut Australia out of major sectors of its market, it could be very painful. If Australia has not taken prudent measures to strengthen resilience, it could be excruciating in the number of businesses ruined and jobs lost. Yet Australia could perhaps take some consolation from the knowledge that it has been through a similar trial. And survived.

When the United Kingdom dumped Australia to join the European Common Market in 1973, it was a profound shock. London cut Australia's longstanding preferential access to the British market and switched all its preferences to Europe instead. In Australia it was widely considered a bitter political betrayal. "In two world wars, New Zealand, Australia and Canada – with India, South Africa and other members of the then Empire – sent thousands upon thousands of troops, airmen and sailors to help save Britain from the Germans," Alexander Downer wrote in London's Telegraph in 2016. "Despite this sacrifice, the attitude of the Heath government in the seventies was 'So what?' ... Doug Anthony, the then deputy prime minister, was so incensed that he abandoned his lifelong support for the Queen in Australia and joined the republican movement." Downer's father, then Australia's high commissioner to London, was devastated. Australia's apple exports fell by 70 per cent, its butter exports by 90 per cent. Any Australian forty-six years old or older lived through the consequences, whether they understood them or not.

Australia didn't just survive. It thrived. Ultimately, by forcing us to compete and survive in the wider world, Britain did Australia a favour. "Australia's abandonment by Britain was the salutary shock that this country needed," economist Oliver Hartwich wrote a few years ago. "Britain may have sought to profit from its turn to Europe, but it was Australia that gained most from it."

All of these are defensive considerations, to protect what Australia already enjoys. But we know that the economic growth of today is running on the fumes of the 1980s and '90s reforms. If Australia hopes to enjoy future long-term growth, it needs new vigour. And that begins with a serious reform program. The Morrison government is in denial about this, because reform is hard and likely to be unpopular, as Hawke and Keating and Howard and Costello found. But it's the essence of political leadership to do what's needed rather than what's convenient. The Reserve Bank governor, Philip Lowe, put it elegantly in an interview: "The best option" for Australia is "creating an environment where firms want to innovate, invest, expand and hire people. I think that's the best option. I'm sure at the analytical level the government would agree. The challenge they have is to develop a program to do that." Anything else is talking points.

Society

Australia has built a Chinese community of 1.2 million people without really understanding it or its consequences. All immigrant communities have strong ties to their home countries. Only one is penetrated by a foreign authoritarian political party with plans to dominate the host country. Australia needs to assist the many Chinese Australians who want to be full participants in their country and deter those who see it as merely a vehicle for serving Beijing's dreams of dominance.

The purposeful enforcement of the foreign interference laws would help. The immigrants who are here because they want to be here, living as Australians, would be freed from pressure from those who do not. As

Professor Feng puts it, "When I came to Australia in 1995, the United Front groups were much less aggressive, but now they aggressively promote this very toxic nationalistic ideology and authoritarian ideology. They force everyone in the Chinese community to take a position – you are our friend or you are our enemy." It's time for Australia to put the same question to the United Front organisers and agents who abuse Australia's democratic freedoms to covertly choke off those freedoms for others.

A review of the immigration mix is timely, too. The composition of the intake of 160,000 foreigners who are accepted each year to settle in Australia is under constant, quiet review by the immigration department. China has been one of the top two source countries in recent years. The department should continue to admit large numbers of ethnic Chinese immigrants. Over Australia's history, most Chinese immigrants have proved to be first-class settlers and citizens. It was Australia's loss to expel them during the White Australia era and the country should never repeat that costly mistake.

Australia has never recovered from the economic consequences of that decision. By driving out all "coloured races," the White Australia policy expelled the greatest force for the development of the northern part of the continent. For example, while Europeans took up the land titles in tropical North Queensland granted after 1876, it was the Chinese settlers who did the arduous work of clearing the heavy tropical jungle so that it could be farmed. They pioneered the banana industry and planted sugar, as well as organising the transport and shipping to get the produce to the cities to the south. It was the Chinese community of North Queensland who provided the capital as well as the labour for regional development, as historian Henry Reynolds documented in his book North of Capricorn. And it was the Chinese who operated the thriving fishing industry of the Cairns region. Years after the Chinese and other "coloureds" had been driven out, it was noted in the Queensland state parliament in 1913 that "the North would be a perfect wilderness today if it had not been for the Chinese opening it up."

The wealthy Chinese merchants in the region were respected local community leaders and important contributors to local life. It was the Chinese immigrants who drove the economy of Darwin, too. "Little or no life appeared" in the European parts of Darwin, while Chinatown was "a welter of life and activity," as a Norwegian scientist, Knut Dahl, observed from a visit in the 1890s. He described the flourishing Chinese families as a "happy" community enjoying life to the full, while the Europeans "very often" sat lonely in their houses or drinking in the public houses, "deploring the fate that had left them stranded on this barren coast."

To this day, northern Australia's underdevelopment is a national frustration, with Canberra trying to engineer activity through the Northern Australia Infrastructure Facility and various subsidies to keep the Northern Territory viable more than a century after vandalising Australia's far north by expelling its dynamic Chinese, Japanese, Pacific Islander, Malay, Filipino and other populations.

When the White Australia laws were under debate in the new national parliament, their sharpest critic, Bruce Smith, the member for Parkes, described them as unnecessary, hysterical and racist. And he left this timeless diagnosis of the mainstream mindset: "Honourable members do not differentiate between acts which may be prevented by legislation, and qualities which are inherent in another people, and on that account make them such great opponents."

Australia today must confront through legislation and other measures the harms exported by the Chinese Communist Party while embracing the remarkable qualities of the Chinese people. Generations of Chinese immigrants have proved to be great contributors to the full spectrum of modern Australia's success. But we have to question the immigration department's success in assessing applicants in recent years. The flourishing United Front activities in Australia are evidence that too many of its organisers and agents are finding a welcome rather than a searching scrutiny. Australia has to protect itself from further easy penetration by people hostile to our democracy. Two protective measures stand out. First is that immigration needs to involve better-qualified officials, from ASIO and Australian diplomatic staff, much more closely in assessing immigrants. This already occurs in some cases. The evidence is that it needs to occur in many more. While the federal government develops the skills and knowledge to winkle out the subversive from the sincere, it should also consider changing the composition in favour of Chinese immigrants from places other than mainland China. Screening must still apply, of course, but prima facie ethnic Chinese immigrants from Taiwan or Hong Kong are more likely to value Australian liberties. This is not an absolute answer, but it is a way to improve the balance of risks, at least until the government is capable of competent screening of people seeking permanent residency and citizenship.

Australia doesn't operate immigration as an act of charity, except in the refugee category. In the main it is operated as a tool of hard-headed national interest It seeks to admit people most suited to the country's needs. Preference should not only be given to immigrants with the most suitable work skills but also to those with the most compatible values. Immigrants who are committed to liberal-democratic principles should always be given priority over those who are not.

World

Australia has already been awakened from a deep torpor to step up its traditional hard power defences. The Rudd government's Defence White Paper promised a major upgrade, including a new fleet of twelve submarines, but was torn up almost immediately by the Gillard government. The Gillard government published a triumphalist Asian Century white paper and cut defence spending to its lowest proportion of GDP since 1939. Gillard did clinch the deal to allow US Marines to operate from the Northern Territory, but decided that free-riding on the United States was all Australia needed to do. The Coalition reversed this blunder and launched a recovery of spending and capability, including the twelve submarines that Rudd first proposed a decade ago.

It's self-evidently a good idea for Australia to have the capacity to defend itself. A full-scale continental invasion is today highly unlikely, but Australia needs to be able to defend its interests, including the vital commercial lifeline of maritime trade, against any threat of interruption, embargo or blockade. The defence minister, Linda Reynolds, is seeking to reform her department, accelerate delivery of major capabilities and invigorate the entire system. China is modernising at high speed and Australia, among others, must try to keep up. "The world has changed more quickly than we assessed in 2016," Senator Reynolds says. She will need the full support of her prime minister and government. Whenever Xi visits a Chinese military base, he dresses in combat uniform and exhorts the troops to prepare to "fight to win." Why would any other country do anything less?

Yet, underprepared as Australia may be, "of all the aspects of national security, defence is the area where we are best prepared," says Jim Molan, the former Australian Army major general who went on to become a Liberal senator. "Australia needs a national security strategy and we don't have one." Molan pressed the Turnbull and Morrison governments to develop one, unsuccessfully. Such a plan would address the need for resilience – including the very basic need for a reserve of fuel. Molan insisted that the government address the fact that Australia has reserves of refined liquid fuels – petrol, diesel, aviation fuel – sufficient to last just three to four weeks in the event of a supply disruption. This compares to the international standard of at least three months' worth. To date, the government response has been to launch an internal inquiry. But fuel is only one aspect. "There's no organisation in Australia that looks across the entire nation and says, 'What are our vulnerabilities – in food, in pharmaceuticals, in water, in energy, in spare parts for missiles and other military equipment?'" says Molan. "Only the prime minister can create one." But that would be if Australia were smart. At the moment it remains dully, obdurately complacent.

Australia has started to wake up to the more modern threat of cyberwarfare. We've seen Russia pioneering it successfully as a seamless extension of traditional war, less visible but utterly lethal, in Georgia and Ukraine, to create a form of "hybrid war." In America, Russia's use of the internet to distract and divide a major power has been awesomely effective and astonishingly easy – consider the turmoil of the Mueller inquiry, Trump's Ukraine phone call and the impeachment hearings.

Cyberwar aims to "cripple a state before that state even realises the conflict has begun," in the words of James Sherr of London's Chatham House research institute. China has built an even more formidable cyber capability. Not content to mount raids on foreign firms and governments, Beijing is engaged in an effort to establish dominance of the entire realm of web-based activity, including warfare capabilities. And as we've seen, according to the responsible US officials, Beijing is winning. When I asked the former head of both the US National Security Agency and Cyber Command, Mike Rogers, what American systems the Russians and Chinese could shut down in the event of a crisis, he answered: "We'll only know when it happens." Australia has to work with the United States on this because it's a highly capable power, but it cannot rely on the US alone. If the United States cannot defend itself successfully against cyber-intrusion, it cannot defend Australia. This is a field where Australia needs to concentrate vastly greater effort and develop unique capability.

The US alliance, as I've argued, is a national asset. It would be unwise to discard it in a time of need. It has never been a security guarantee – that is a fond fiction Australia's political class has talked itself into believing, a fiction that cannot survive a reading of the actual treaty. Donald Trump has politicised US alliances, adding a new level of uncertainty to American reliability. And, of course, he's added his own personal touch of erraticism. Yet the alliance nonetheless is a vital asset for supplying intelligence, hardware and technology, even in peacetime. And at a time of war, the alliance, at the very least, must complicate any enemy's hostile calculations.

One indicator of the value of the US alliance is how keen the Chinese government is to break it. The US alliance system of some forty countries is an American advantage that China cannot match. Beijing has "a strategy of picking off the smaller ones first," as Rudd puts it, and has had some success with New Zealand already. Rudd is the only Australian who has spent extended time with Xi Jinping. In 2010, as prime minister, he hosted Xi, then a vice premier of China, for several days at the Lodge. The two had some six or seven extended conversations, recalls Rudd, mostly one-on-one in Mandarin. Rudd says that he set out three central features of Australia for Xi.

First was that it's a Western, liberal democracy. "We believe in universal human rights, and that's not going to change." Second was that "we are a US ally, and that's not going to change." Third was that Australia and China had been allies during World War II, and that the two countries could again work closely together. "It was a realist framework — here are two constraints, and here is a field of opportunity," he tells me. "Within those two constraints, we should work together as vigorously as possible." Xi's response, according to Rudd, was "complete comprehension." Yet not acquiescence. Rudd says that Beijing doesn't think it's likely that Australia will abandon its alliance with Washington, but it will never stop working towards that aim.

Professor Shi Yinhong of Renmin University, an informal adviser to China's leadership, told me that it would be "an undreamed-of luxury" for Beijing if Australia were to sever its alliance with the United States.

Beijing likes to arrange other countries into concentric circles of assessed priority. It has partners, strategic partners, comprehensive strategic partners, and so on. At the very pinnacle it has one "all-weather strategic cooperative partner," a status reserved for Pakistan alone. As Scott Morrison recently boasted, Australia is categorised as a "comprehensive strategic partner" of China. True. But this year, Papua New Guinea, Kazakhstan and the United Arab Emirates, among others, were elevated to the same status. In 2018 Zimbabwe was, too. New Zealand and Brazil are in the club. All of the European Union has been there for over a decade. Xi has suggested that the entire continent of Africa could be as well.

Geremie Barmé calls Beijing's "endless slicing of the world into this relationship matrix" a series of "Dante-like circles." In reality, he says, the underlying calculus is "who are our allies, who can be potentially won over, who can't be won over, who are our enemies." And "being labelled strategic by China means, 'You've got shit we want.'" Fellow Sinologist Anne-Marie Brady lists the main attractions Australia holds for China: "Australia represents access to strategic mineral resources, [is] a source of agricultural produce, wields significant political influence in the South Pacific and Antarctic governances, is a member of the Five Eyes intelligence network, a NATO partner state, a close ally of the USA through ANZUS, an influential medium power in the global system and especially in the Asia-Pacific region, where China seeks to dominate." These are all Australian assets that Beijing would like to turn to its advantage.

She also lists the negatives that Beijing would like to neutralise: "Australia has a significant navy engaging in freedom of navigation operations in the South China Sea, Australia has a role in China's Belt and Road agenda, and the Australian federal government's public opposition to Belt and Road and Huawei frustrates China's global agenda. Australia's actions to address China's foreign interference activities are a model to the rest of the world and many of Australia's partners and friends are now going through the same assessment process which led to Australia's new laws." All of this, the positives and the negatives, are sources of Australian power and influence.

When Australia has toughened itself against the CCP's attempts at interference and control, it will be much better able to work confidently and energetically with the Chinese government. And it should. There is strong mutual benefit in advancing trade and investment, between the two nations directly, but also in salvaging the international economic system from US assault. Australia and China would benefit from working together in health services and education, finance and technology, in mitigating climate change, and in cooperating to lift living standards in the Pacific Islands. And from working together to defeat transnational harms — drug trafficking, people trafficking, piracy and terrorism, for instance. And there is a big, rich arena for shared enjoyment of sport and culture.

The man Bob Hawke turned to thirty years ago to spur Australia's engagement with a rising China today describes the logical consequence now that China is risen: "There was always going to be systemic competition between a rich China and the US-led West," says Ross Garnaut. "The pull of each of the pole stars depends on how attractive each turns out to be for its own citizens and for people everywhere." Unfortunately, the US-led West isn't looking its best at the moment, and that's a liability for the democratic world. "History," says Garnaut, "has weighted the scales against democracy at the critical time. The systemic competition is coming to a head when the US and the democratic West are less attractive than they have been for many generations." He cites the fact that the US president is "condemning the globalisation and the respect for knowledge upon which our prosperity and democracy depend." He points to the economic inadequacies of the United States and Australia: "Stagnant living standards for ordinary citizens over four decades in the US and half a dozen years in Australia." He doesn't for a moment propose that Australia break with the US alliance to join Pakistan as Beijing's second "all-weather strategic cooperative partner." He prescribes that "a successful, democratic Australia requires a close and productive relationship with China, alongside our deep and strong relationship with the US, and a rich relationship with the other great powers of Asia. There is no peace, no prosperity and no climate stability without making a global economy and polity work." The elements of that include deep understanding of others, respect for alternative views, close communications, and preparedness to adjust to changing realities abroad as well as at home. "This is as true now as it was when I started following the Chinese reforms four decades ago. Developments in the domestic politics of all of our great and powerful friends have made that more difficult. That makes it even more important that Australians get it right."

This is his central message. Garnaut stresses the primacy of Australia succeeding in its own right. "The most important thing that we can do is make our own democracy work for all Australians. That means unshackling policy from foreign and vested interests, to allow government in the public interest." This involves shutting out the lobbyists and special favours and implementing a federal ICAC to investigate police corruption, as well as shutting down China's relentless efforts at covert manipulation, political interference and cyber-intrusion. Ross Garnaut says that the result of his son's handiwork is just a starting point: "The anti-interference legislation, which was not directed only against China, was an important step. It has to be taken much further."

Australia needs to concentrate on strengthening itself, making itself armour-plated against foreign subversion, so that it can engage confidently with China and the world, because it cannot count on anyone else. Australia is best served when democracy is thriving everywhere, but with a global democratic recession now entering its fourteenth year, we have to be prepared to face a world where it is in retreat everywhere. Australia has to be prepared to go it alone if necessary. History is forcing us out of our complacency. Whenever Australia is asked to choose between China and America, the ultimate answer must be that we choose Australia.

Correspondence

Grant Marjoribanks

Sam was six in 2014, when I was planning my return to work after several months recovering from a heart transplant. He overheard me on the phone one day as I arranged a meeting.

"Who was that, Dad?"

"That's Fiona from work."

"Are you going back to work?"

"Yeah."

"Oh, that's terrible news!"

"Why's that, mate?"

"Because you've already got a job."

"What's that?"

"Being my dad."

Why are your children so uniquely capable of observations that invoke both joy and guilt at the same time?

Annabel Crabb clearly understands that species of guilt that is the constant, silent – and sometimes not so silent – companion of the modern working father. Guilt that you're not doing your share of child-raising tasks, guilt that you're not 100 per cent dedicated to your job, guilt that you're not the wise, playful, funny, ever-present omni-dad.

What struck me about *Men at Work* was the depth of Crabb's understanding. Of men. And in a sphere of human behaviour where judgment, of men, could be entirely justified. As Crabb notes, "It's well established that having children is entirely different, when it comes to your professional outlook, depending on whether you're male or female ... Any study you like in this area will show you that the same biological event – reproduction – means strikingly different things for men at work as opposed to women."

Crabb rightly notes that social policy and expectations around child-raising have a disproportionate impact on the career and financial prospects of women. That is a central issue here. But it is not the only issue, and she sensitively acknowledges how social policy and expectations also discriminate against men, and thereby work to the detriment of children.

Crabb gets it.

She gets that for some men, sometimes, those social expectations will be quietly convenient. "Now, no one is suggesting that what every dad really wants to do," she writes, "is get home from work at 4 p.m. every day so as to be sure to catch that excellent juncture where the juvenile and the adult stores of patience expire within fifteen minutes of each other. When I first read Edith Gray's research indicating that the average Australian father worked five hours more a week after the birth of his first child, somewhere deep down inside I grinned in recognition and thought: you sly dogs."

Okay, she got me there. I took a two-week "break" after both Sam and Jude were born (although I don't remember smoking any cigars). In the early years of their lives, I changed my share of nappies. I staggered out of bed for many middle-of-the-night bottles. I clocked kilometres pushing a pram anxiously around local streets in the vague hope that it would calm my shrieking child. But did I put my hand up for the "unrecompensed crapshoot" of several months of parental leave? Hell no.

Crabb also gets that, for some men, sometimes, those expectations will cut deep. "Somehow we've constructed a system of expectations … in which a man who is doing his job is bound to it by something much deeper and more fibrous than his contract of employment, or even his need to provide. Stopping work for a while, or even just doing less of it, is thus not as simple as a law telling him it's allowed. It involves finding and loosening restraints far more ancient than those outlined in any human resources manual; knots which have swelled with age and seawater; ropes that have bitten into the skin."

She really got me there, right in the heart of my personal narrative.

I did go back to work in 2014, and soon started to thrive professionally. But the more I succeeded in one job, the less adequate I felt in the other.

In 2017, work commitments frequently took me away from home, and even when I was there, I wasn't. I started every weekday with an 8 a.m. conference call, switching the phone on and off mute as I made school lunches, packed school bags, barked commands, buttoned shirts, combed hair, broke up fights, got involved in fights, barked more commands and whispered hurried goodbyes at drop-off. I was constantly checking email, from before the boys woke up until well after they had gone to bed. One family "holiday" coincided with a particularly hectic period, and I spent the whole time on my phone. I would go to the bathroom to buy five minutes to clear some of my email backlog. During one beachside walk, with me trailing ten metres behind, glued to my phone, Sam lost it.

"I hate this holiday," he declared. "You're always on your phone, you don't pay any attention to us. I want to go home."

Since that time, my sense of work–family conflict has become more pronounced. Clocks are ticking and I am increasingly feeling an urgent need to be more present in my boys' lives. Sam is now eleven, Jude eight – crucial dad time for the fathers of boys. Steve Biddulph's advice and warning is etched in my mind: "This window of time – from about age six to the fourteenth birthday – is the major opportunity for a father to have an influence on (and build the foundations of masculinity in) his son. Now is the time to 'make time' … This is when good memories are laid down, which will nourish your son, and you, for decades to come … Enjoy this time when he is really wanting to be with you. By mid-adolescence his interests will pull him more and more into the wider world beyond. All I can do here is plead with you – don't leave it too late!"

So for some time I have been keeping a log in my mind, doing the calculations. When will I reach the point that Max Schireson did, the Silicon Valley CEO who stepped down from his role because the demands of his job meant he wasn't spending enough time with his fourteen-, twelve- and nine-year-old children? As my wife put it recently, echoing Biddulph, "The boys don't need you in four or five years' time. They need you now." Just as my sense of work–family conflict hit extreme on hearing those words, she released the pressure valve with her next observation: "Why don't you try going part-time for a while?"

The idea should not have been the revelation that it was to me. So why had I been seeing my situation as an either/or dilemma until that point?

I am particularly prone to the male tendency to describe and identify myself with reference to work. I also imagine the voices of the 24/7 types – those types who, when my firm formally adopted a flexible working policy many years ago, coined the derogatory term "part-time partner." In the end, though, with the support of an encouraging wife, enlightened managers, sympathetic colleagues and a talented and dedicated team, I prioritised the little voices that really matter. Sam's and Jude's.

I have two jobs. I may have allowed one to become more important to me than the other at a key stage in my own and my boys' lives, but both are important. And slowly I am becoming optimistic that de-throttling in one may ultimately improve my chances of thriving in both.

Thank you, Annabel Crabb, for getting it.

Grant Marjoribanks

Maddison Connaughton

I returned to Figure 1 many times as I moved through this essay, enough for the spine to soften along the crease at that point. Now I often find the text falls open naturally at that page. It would be a shame if this graph were the only thing a reader took away from Annabel Crabb's skewering *Men at Work* – but, my god, this graph. Has there been a more effective visual aid in the history of the *Quarterly Essay*? It would be a fitting laurel for an essay that finds much of its power in seeing what others have missed, or avoided, or ignored.

The mother's time-use survey is still striking, even now. It has a sort of gravitational pull – such a perfect distillation of the fear many young women hold close about having children. "The graph itself looks like the heart rate of a very, very stressed person," writes Crabb. Or someone who has been struck by lightning.

I don't have any children, although the statistics suggest I will in the next few years. By their early thirties, two-thirds of women in Australia will have at least one child. At this age, only one in five women will work full-time, contrasted with four out of five of their male peers. See Figure 1.

As I read this essay, though, I found myself looking increasingly to the corresponding graph, which traces how the father's life adapts to having a child, how it barely shifts over the course of twelve years – resolutely impervious to change. Initially, I was racked by jealousy. Of course men will refuse to bend, to soften along the spine when something as cataclysmic as a child comes into their life. And yet, in the end, I came to see the father's timeline as utterly dull. A twelve-year holding pattern stretching out who knows how far in either direction.

Clearly, the turbulence mothers experience isn't preferable. But ultimately, the question I couldn't shake was why this was the system we built. Why build a something to make ourselves miserable?

Australia's paid parental leave scheme began in 2011, not 1970. Already there was a wealth of research to hand and international precedent for something better-constructed. There was an understanding of how interruption to women's working lives feeds into the gender pay gap and the superannuation gap. It had been sixteen years since the influential journal *Feminist Economics* launched. At the same time, Australia – having weathered the global financial crisis relatively unscathed – saw its female labour participation rate for those aged twenty-five to fifty-four drop *below 75 per cent*. For men, the rate remained above 90 per cent.

Yet we enacted one of the least generous paid parental leave schemes in the OECD. Is this truly the best that was politically possible? So much in the carelessness of parental leave makes you wonder who was in the room when the policy was formulated.

Before reading this essay, I had never been on a "mum and bub" forum, though I promptly found myself tumbling into an internet rabbit hole. They are fascinating spaces: an entire underground economy of mothers trading advice about how to navigate Australia's rigid parental leave system.

The lessons are myriad but, for now, just two.

First, no one should have ever let Joe Hockey walk into that interview with Laurie Oakes and use the term "double-dipping" to describe mothers who seek to access both public parental leave and a private scheme offered by their employer. Years on, these forums still seethe at the term. There are threads, hundreds of comments deep, replete with mothers venting their frustration about the political ignorance that allowed "double-dipping" to end up among a treasurer's talking points. Mothers upbraiding this system that frames having a child as a burden to the taxpayer, rather than a public good.

The other key point is that mothers are highly organised. Not in the "everything in its place" sense, but in the tightly networked, informed, constantly communicating way that can sway public sentiment. The kind of community that political campaigns dream of tapping into.

And it does make you wonder who's in the room – when "double-dipping" gets signed off as a talking point, when eighteen weeks at minimum wage is seen as the best option that is politically possible, when the need to reform a system that devalues female labour is ignored for nearly a decade.

Perhaps now, when – as Crabb points out – both our prime minister and our treasurer are the fathers of young children, there is an opportunity for improvement. A chance to soften the rigidity in the system. Perhaps the economic headwinds that Australia faces will render a more generous leave scheme an attractive option for stimulus by another name. One only needs to look at the positive response to Cricket Australia's twelve-month paid parental leave scheme to see there is appetite in the community for something better.

Clearly our policy-makers need to think more inclusively, to view new parents and their child as a unit – and allow them to figure out what works best for their particular circumstances. To give families the choice to divvy up a block of leave – at least twenty weeks, though ideally more – between both parents, and to consider a "use it or lose it" minimum for each.

It would be hard for a reader to come away from this essay without the sense that parental leave shapes so many things in our society. That if policy-makers were to take the macro view – as Crabb has done so effectively – they would see how expensive and apparently intractable issues could be moved by a better approach. Workforce participation, mental health and gender equality – something we know is key to reducing gendered violence – are just the first that come to mind.

But on questions of family, perhaps more than any other subject, our search for answers too often shrinks to the personal, the anecdotal. What other parents managed to pull off, or where they failed. When I finished this essay, the first thing I did was text my dad. I asked him how much leave he took when I was born. "Hi!" came his reply, immediately. "I don't think I took any carer's leave. I was there when you were born though. It wasn't really an option, as far as I know. I still think it's low (5 per cent?). Why do you ask?"

Maddison Connaughton

Angela Shanahan

Last year I wrote a column inspired by the imminent birth of the baby of
New Zealand's prime minister, Jacinda Ardern. I mused that it might be difficult
to be a breastfeeding mother and prime minister, even of New Zealand. Babies
are naturally bonded to their mothers. Indeed, bonding is part of the natural
biological imperative of breastfeeding. But Ardern had announced that she would
only take six weeks' leave before passing "parenting" to the child's father. Well,
good luck with that one, I said, because she needed a lot more time off.

The responses I received were pretty virulent, and mostly from various
high-powered female types. How dare I criticise the feminist pin-up of the
Southern Hemisphere! A woman can have a baby and a job! Well, yes. I know
that. I had to do it, and so did my mother, and in both cases it was a matter of
dire necessity.

Left-leaning feminist commentators on family issues often can't see past the
flaws in the ideological symbolism to the simple everyday practical realities: like
new mothers having to *learn* to breastfeed and wanting to bond with babies; or
what happens at home when the father simply can't be there, because despite all
the hype and wishful thinking on the part of feminists, men are still the main
earners in most Australian families.

Annabel Crabb's *Men at Work*, which quotes my view of Jacinda as part of the
mindset of the "parenthood trap," is basically about why fathers aren't mothers.
It is a long complaint about fathers not taking parental leave.

It is curious that she uses the word "trap." Why is it a trap to be a mother or
father? Why is it so important, as she seems to think, to get out?

Perhaps, despite her artfully recherché image with matching culinary accom-
plishments, Crabb can't stand the heat in the everyday meat-and-potatoes kitchen.
Like most of the women — and it is mostly women — who comment on this stuff,
she betrays a somewhat scornful attitude to the hard yakka of the domestic front.

Many women are understandably resentful of the grubby everyday domestic necessities: the washing and cleaning; the cooking; the changing of the nappies; putting one foot in front of the other through the zombie like days of three-hourly feeds; not to mention that when children are sick, upset or in trouble, it is always Mummy who is expected to be on the frontline. First-time mothers often don't understand all of this, and they often need much longer leave than they can get; and naturally, they don't want to do it alone. But someone has to do it, and Crabb seems to think that men taking more paternity leave is the solution.

Her thesis is that women's exit from dreary domesticity into the workplace (often just as dreary) is not matched by an exit from work by men to support the poor overburdened women. Why should men want to be out of work? The plain truth is that in most Australian families, no amount of take-it-or-leave-it paternity leave or any other inducement will change these arrangements, because most families are still dependent primarily on the father's earnings, as they have a whopping big mortgage. The family enterprise depends on the main breadwinner, who is usually the man. The consequence of this is that in most families, even if the father takes paternity leave, it is only for a short period. Since nature equipped women to be mothers, and most will take maternity leave, it is imperative, especially if mothers have a long time off, that fathers don't.

Of course, it doesn't make it any emotionally easier for men. Crabb interviewed Scott Morrison and Josh Frydenberg about their family life, which she says is all about "coping with and compensating for absence" and asks, "Why do we expect so little of fathers"? Who says it is "little"? Anyone who observes these men at close quarters knows that what they do is not little. In fact, it is good that they are aware enough to want to manage absence. What is wrong with that? Crabb seems oblivious to the reality of being prime minister and treasurer. Does she think that their wives holding the fort at home is wrong, because it makes it practically easier for these two men, or any man, to do their jobs? Dads should share, but often they just simply can't. And never mind about the prime minister — ask any tradie trying to build up their business.

What really upsets the commentators is that the general population dismisses the impractical pretence that a father can be a mother, hence the handy gender-neutral term "parenting," which smothers the difference. That there is a difference between "mother" and "father" doesn't mean that fathers should not be involved with their children. On the contrary: it is absolutely vital that they are. However, their involvement is different from the mother's. And sometimes that difference is qualitative, and can't be measured in time.

Actually, the best way that fathers can be involved with children is to be involved with their mothers. But in the fractured social milieu, where the natural biological bonds of parents and children have been frayed by family disintegration and gender ideologues who would like to obliterate them completely, we have forgotten that good parenting is actually *a function of* a good marriage.

As far as the solution to the "work–life balance," as it is sometimes called, the availability of maternity leave and part-time work is a boon for Australian mothers, who have never been keen on full-time work with small children, even mothers with highly paid careers. Two of my daughters – who have five children between them – have been able to take extended maternity leave, and through their generous leave and part-time work provisions have been able to continue their careers, including gaining seniority. But they are fortunate, and not all women can do this. Many first-time mothers I have spoken to, who are usually over thirty when they finally have "the baby," are not keen to return to the drudgery of work at all.

My own upbringing and experience as a mother of nine children taught me that the ordinary suburban world is full of many different families whose priorities are usually centred on their children's welfare, while trying to juggle their finances as best they can. But the family is not an ideological construct built around economics. It doesn't always fit into sociological models. It is a natural thing of flesh and blood. That is why if you ask anyone, male or female, which is more important for a mother, getting back to work or cultivating a warm and lasting maternal bond with her infant child, I think I know which they would choose.

Angela Shanahan

Marian Baird

Annabel Crabb has a gift for identifying topical matters and writing about them in a witty and knowledgeable way: paid paternity leave is one such zeitgeist issue. In *Men at Work*, she unpacks the three forces that shape Australian approaches to fatherhood and work: flexism, sexism and masculinism. Flexism occurs because flexible work practices should be available to all but are mainly used by women; sexism occurs because Australia's paid parental leave scheme prioritises mothers; and masculinism is seen where societal and workplace cultures and practices reward men for working long hours rather than spending time with their family. I've been studying these patterns for two decades and it's true that fathers, in the main, work longer hours and receive higher pay than mothers, or people of either gender without children. The biggest pay gap is between working fathers and working mothers. New mothers often shift to part-time work and thereafter the pay gap, care gap, hours gap and superannuation gap are compounded.

The Australian Women's Working Futures survey showed that young working parents desire more equitable gender relations, both at home and at work. Young families with a mother and a father want policies that enable both parents to take leave from work and maintain their careers. They want support such as paid parental leave and quality childcare. Young women without children also consider these policies important. But here's my concern: young men in the labour market without children do not have the same expectations. They are not factoring in future work–family tensions, which means they are probably not pushing for parental leave. And that's where I think *Men at Work* has missed part of the problem.

Twenty years ago, I started researching Australia's lack of paid maternity leave because I was outraged that we didn't have a scheme for all working women – and yet women were nonetheless expected to go to work and have children. I examined the historical antecedents of Australia's leave model, which was embedded in its industrial relations system, not its social security scheme. The introduction in 1973 by Whitlam of twelve weeks' paid maternity leave for federal public servants was a breakthrough. It was unique and unprecedented. Contrary to what Crabb writes, it was not picked up quickly by the private sector.

In 1979, Bob Hawke, then leader of the Australian Council of Trade Unions (ACTU), directed the peak body's first female research officer, Jan Marsh, to run the inaugural maternity leave test case. The task was enormous. It resulted in the Industrial Relations Commission (IRC), forerunner of the Fair Work Commission, awarding fifty-two weeks' unpaid maternity leave and a job guarantee, the latter being critical to the real value of the leave scheme. In subsequent test cases taken up by the ACTU, this type of leave was extended to adoptive parents, and later to working fathers. Following a further application by the ACTU in 1990, the IRC renamed it "parental leave" and made it available to all parents, fathers and mothers.

It was not until 1993 that parental leave was enshrined in industrial legislation rather than awards; the entitlement now sits in the *Fair Work Act*, as one of our National Employment Standards. However, parental leave was, and remains, unpaid. Because employers would have vigorously opposed paid leave in the test cases all those years ago, the decision was made by the ACTU to demand the right to job protection and let parental leave remain unpaid.

Our current *paid* parental leave system came about by a somewhat different route. During the 1990s, forces were gathering to introduce paid maternity leave for working women. This benefit had been on the agenda before – for example, during the Accord years – but it had never been won. In 1996, Senator Natasha Stott Despoja of the Australian Democrats put forward an amendment to the Workplace Relations Bill to introduce paid maternity leave for private sector employees. In 2002, Pru Goward, as sex discrimination commissioner, released her proposal for a national paid maternity leave scheme. Then, during the 2000s, the campaign rapidly gathered momentum and women from the community and not-for-profit sectors supported it, while the Young Women's Christian Association, the ACTU, women trade unionists and women on the street demanded it. From the late 1990s, a band of female academics, including me, had been researching, advocating and presenting conference papers and submissions supporting the need for paid maternity leave. Jenny Macklin in the Labor Party, Heather Ridout, head of the Australian Industry Group, and Liz Broderick, the sex discrimination commissioner at the time, strongly supported the model.

The case for Labor to request a Productivity Commission inquiry on the matter was made just before the 2007 election by Marie Coleman of the National Foundation for Australian Women, and the argument was taken up by the party. As incoming Labor prime minister, Kevin Rudd finally introduced Australia's paid parental leave scheme in 2010, but it was the time-consuming and demanding campaigning of so many women for over a decade that led to this turning point. The result would not have come about without the efforts and dedication of these women, and many more I have not mentioned.

In 2014, Liberal Party MPs Joe Hockey and Scott Morrison sought to attack the scheme and undermine its architecture. They called women "rorters," "fraudsters" and "double dippers" for exercising their right to access the government's minimum-pay benefit supplemented with pay from their employers, where that opportunity existed. Once again, women had to stand up for themselves and mount a campaign to save the system. Once again, it fell to women to fight for paid parental leave. Thankfully, the scheme celebrates its tenth birthday next year. There are aspects of it that should be improved, such as an increase in assistance to single mothers, the addition of superannuation and its flexibility, but the scheme survives.

Back to fathers and paternity leave, the focus of Crabb's essay. In its 2009 report, the Productivity Commission's inquiry also recommended introducing paternity leave pay. Did I see men advocating for this? Not in great numbers. When it was omitted from the final design for fiscal reasons, did I see men argue for it? No. When the Dad and Partner Pay amendment was introduced in 2013, giving men up to two weeks of government-funded pay, did I see men in the streets celebrating its arrival? I don't think so. Do I now see men forming committees, organising through their social networks and union groups, speaking up at work, arguing for more time to look after their children? I see some, but not many.

I hope Crabb's timely essay inspires more men – fathers, sons, brothers, grandfathers and fathers-to-be – to organise and campaign for more paid paternity leave so that they take time out of work to look after their children. I hope it inspires working men around Australia to argue with their employers for flexible work options to care for their family members, young and old. I hope men join the cause to improve our public policies for all. With men on board this campaign, we will start to see the changes in flexism, sexism and masculinism – and the possibility of gender equality in the struggle for work–life balance – that today's young parents want to achieve.

Marian Baird

Andrew Wear

As the father of young children, I find the scenarios Annabel Crabb presents all too familiar. In public settings, some people seem to regard fathers attending to their children as remarkable rather than routine. When my children were infants, it was disconcerting to be patronised with congratulations ("Aren't you good?") for the mere act of looking after them. In the workplace and online, discussions focus on the challenges for women of balancing work and family. They rarely seem to involve men; the implicit – and infuriating – assumption being that men don't face the same challenge. Given many men are engaged in a day-to-day struggle to stay upright as they attempt to balance work with parenting and being a responsible partner, I suspect men need to do a better job of creating spaces to talk about this.

It's easy to understand why Crabb is taken with the idea of a "daddy quota" as part of an enhanced parental leave system. Recently, I interviewed a number of people in Iceland about their experiences of gender equality and was amazed to learn that Icelandic men take an *average* of eighty-seven days of paternity leave after the birth of each child. Picture almost every fisherman, lawyer or construction worker spending months away from work caring for their child, and you get a sense of how transformative this is. While their partner returns to work, these men are pushing prams, at the playground or at home, cleaning and changing nappies. Imagine what that means for how their families function.

The discussion in Iceland is now focused on a further extension of paid parental leave to twelve months. The government has agreed that this will be implemented between 2020 and 2021, although the detail is still being resolved. One option being considered is that each parent may be given five months of leave, with the remaining two months to share.

There's a big evidence base demonstrating that parenting behaviour established at childbirth tends to persist as children age. Parental leave arrangements are undoubtedly critical in laying the foundations for parenting equality. But parental leave in the first year of a child's life is not enough. Parenting is a long game, and we need to consider how we support parents throughout the entire life course.

Crabb does us all a great service by shining a light on the gendered assumptions that underpin the notion of the "primary parent," which is built into much of our policy. Yet the primary parent would not be possible without its inverse: the primary worker. Many policy settings still harbour an implicit assumption that one parent – usually a man – is working full-time to provide for their family. There's a long history of this in Australia, dating back to the Harvester judgment of 1907, in which the Commonwealth Court of Conciliation and Arbitration proclaimed that a minimum wage should be paid to a male worker that is sufficient to provide for a wife and three children. While we've since moved in the direction of gender-neutral pay structures, the assumption of the primary worker lives on in the practical way that work is structured. A standard working week might be thirty-eight hours, but in practice full-time work in Australia mostly involves working for more than forty hours per week. According to the OECD, about 60 per cent of Australian men work longer than forty hours each week. By contrast, about half of Australian women work part-time (thirty-four hours or less) and fewer than 30 per cent work more than forty hours. This is one reason women are paid almost $500 – or about 31 per cent – less each week than men, as recent ABS data reports.

Crabb envisions a world in which domestic work is shared equally between both parents. She rightfully points out that this is what a new generation of parents are often striving to achieve. Yet if we are to move away from the assumption of the "primary parent," I posit that we also need to dismantle the assumption of the primary worker. If the fatigued and stressed parents at my daughters' primary school are any indication, full-time work as a parent seems possible only if there's another person to pick up the load at home at least some of the time. Equality is unlikely to be achieved with both parents working forty hours or more each week. This has the potential to drive families to breaking point. Rather, to achieve greater domestic equality, increase female workforce participation and move closer to equal pay, fathers will need to spend less time at work and more time at home. According to the OECD, in countries where unpaid labour is more equally shared, there tend to be smaller gender-specific differences in hours spent in the workplace.

Spending less time at work may mean men working part-time or more flexibly, as Crabb suggests, but it should also include a consideration of how we can reduce the hours associated with full-time work in Australia. Annual working hours in Australia are by no means the longest in the developed world (that honour goes to Mexico), but the average Australian worker spends 249 hours more at work each year than workers in Norway – the poster child in Crabb's essay. This is the equivalent of an additional six weeks each year. In Norway, hardly anyone works for more than forty hours per week, strict working hours of 8 a.m. to 4 p.m. are common, and overtime is limited by law. Five weeks of annual leave is standard. Under these conditions, and with childcare heavily subsidised, it's possible to see how a shared work and home life might be achievable. Aside from greater potential to balance the demands of work and home, reduced working hours have other benefits too. Countries with fewer annual hours worked tend to have higher labour productivity. It seems that stress, fatigue and sleep deprivation may make overworked employees substantially less productive. Who would have thought?

It is somewhat surprising that Crabb doesn't really consider the gender pay gap in her analysis. The answer to the question of who works and who stays at home involves a complex calculus, worked through within each family. No doubt cultural and identity factors are relevant, but families also consider the financial implications of various decisions, including the cost of childcare and the wages earned by each parent. Even when working full-time, Australian women earn 11.7 per cent less than men, on average. With most Australian fathers earning more than mothers, and at a life stage when every dollar is tight, it's no real surprise that a majority of Australian families choose to send the father off to work.

For this equation to change, real progress in tackling the gender pay gap is required. Australia's performance in this area has been fairly dismal. In twenty years, the gap in full-time earnings has decreased only marginally, from 13.2 per cent in 1998 to 11.7 per cent in 2018. Over the same time period, other countries have done much better. Belgium has reduced the gap in full-time earnings from 15.2 per cent to 3.7 per cent, and this hasn't happened accidentally. With strong trade union membership, 96 per cent of workers are covered by collective bargaining agreements, making it nearly impossible to pay women less to do the same job. The Belgian government has mandated that the gender pay gap be taken into account when wage agreements are negotiated. And all companies with more than fifty employees have to report publicly on their gender pay gap.

Crabb was right to focus on the need for fathers to play a greater role in parenting. As she suggests, we need to do more to ensure that parents are able to share the load at work and at home. Other countries show us that it can be done. With sufficient determination and a concerted effort, it's possible in Australia too.

Andrew Wear

	Correspondence

Mark Tennant

Annabel Crabb makes an overdue appeal for us to consider the "other side of the equation" of gendered work and family life. She poses the question: "What happens to men when they have kids?" In the context of heterosexual married couples, she proceeds to address the barriers men face if they truly wish to engage in work and family life as equals with their partner. Of course, she is mindful of what happens to women – how their careers suffer, and how they bear the brunt of parenting, childcare and household work; how gendered expectations unfairly subject working mothers to interrogations about how they cope with work and family life (but typically exempt fathers). So why focus on men? Well, Crabb puts the case that women will benefit from changes in the workplace attitudes and policies that hinder men's engagement with family life. We learn, for example, that men are twice as likely to be refused flexible working arrangements as women, that men take up only a tiny fraction of available primary-carer leave provisions, that stay-at-home dads are isolated in the community and that workplaces are more accepting of the family demands placed on mothers than on fathers.

By highlighting the systemic barriers men face in gaining access to domestic work, Crabb is changing the terms of the debate. This is actually quite a radical departure. Hitherto, the primary focus has been on women.

Crabb seems a tad concerned that, in shifting the focus, she is entering into dangerous territory – hence her reassurances that she is not for one minute forgetting the well-documented disadvantages faced by women.

Doubtless for some, this refocusing on men is laughable – surely the evidence is that men don't seek such access? But such a dismissive attitude is arguably the result of a highly gendered view of the value of paid as opposed to unpaid domestic work. Paid work is seen as a source of self-worth, identity, financial security and productive engagement with others, while unpaid domestic work is typically seen as simply a list of chores to be completed. This devaluing of unpaid labour is apparent, at least implicitly, in research and media reports on the unfair burden placed on women and the call for men to do their "share." In contrast, mothers' smaller share of paid work is regarded as a barrier to full participation and access.

The Australian Institute of Family Studies reports that the total (paid and unpaid) weekly work hours of (heterosexual) married couples with children are roughly the same, with fathers working seventy-five hours per week and mothers working seventy-seven hours per week. However, the distribution of labour in these arrangements is such that women undertake fewer paid work hours and many more unpaid work hours than men. This is frequently portrayed as a systemic issue that disadvantages women – and it is. But Crabb is making the case that it also disadvantages men who want to be more engaged in family life but have "long work hours, lack of flexibility" and difficulty accessing "family-related leave."

Crabb cites a number of policy initiatives in other countries that promote men's engagement with family life, most notably in Norway, Iceland, Germany and the province of Quebec, in Canada. And she identifies a number of initiatives of businesses in Australia. However, while she acknowledges the overriding influence of cultural assumptions in shaping gendered roles, she focuses mainly on the paid-work dimension and misses an opportunity to dissect further the gendered nature of unpaid work.

Research conducted by Stephanie Wiesmann in the Netherlands (published in the journal *Community, Work and Family*) provides some insight into this. She and others posed the questions, "Who is responsible for seeing that domestic tasks are carried out?", "Who carries out which tasks?" and "To what standard are the tasks performed and how frequently?" The answers are hardly surprising. Even among those who share domestic work equally, the tasks undertaken clearly indicated a gendered division of labour. For example, laundry was done by women, while men did household repairs. Moreover, women were typically the household managers, often delegating tasks to their partners and supervising their work. They determined who did what and to what standard. Men were typically passive, waiting to be told what to do, with some resenting close supervision and reacting to it by withdrawing. Those women who preferred to do tasks themselves often referred to their expertise and their partner's lack of expertise. For example, one woman said her partner didn't take into account clothing labels when doing laundry, and did not stack the dishwasher properly (the list could go on: the need to separate colours for the washing machine, hanging clothes out to dry using the correct peg technique, carefully selecting children's clothes to wear to a party, handwashing valuable crockery, folding laundry in the correct manner, wiping surfaces with the appropriate cloth and spray).

Numerous studies over many years outline the gendered nature of the distribution of household tasks. The household management role assumed by women is attributed to the higher standards they demand, because their identity is invested in the domestic sphere, which is generally not the case with men. It seems, then, that the domestic sphere is a mirror image of the paid workforce, where men are overwhelmingly the managers (as Crabb's essay states, women comprise only "10 per cent of executives and 6 per cent of CEOs in the ASX200"). If it is accepted that men need to cede power to women in the paid workplace, is it reasonable to expect women to cede power to men in the domestic workplace? Is the role of women in the domestic workplace a barrier to men's access and participation? These questions are at least worth posing, and they are certainly questions raised by Crabb's essay.

Mark Tennant

Andrew Thackrah

There aren't many of us, apparently. Or at least not nearly as many as there could be.

It's a Thursday – my regular day off to care for my one-year-old daughter – and during a nap time of unpredictable length I'm reading Annabel Crabb's *Men at Work*. Crabb's essay reveals just how far we are from anything approaching gender equality when it comes to caring for our own offspring. As more and more women with kids have joined the workforce, men simply haven't picked up the household slack. Crabb notes that in Australian families with at least one child under twelve, more than 40 per cent of mothers work part-time. The figure for fathers is only 4 per cent.

It is clear, though, that Australian men want to dedicate more time to raising their children, as Crabb argues. The strength of her analysis is in pointing to the stubborn attitudes that act as a handbrake on that change. Taxpayer-funded parental leave is seen as easy money, and flexible work is seen as something you get away with (rather than a necessity). More than a quarter of men actually experience discrimination when they return to work after taking leave for the birth of a child – this kind of "soft" work is still associated with women.

One of the things that struck me while reading *Men at Work* is that any discussion of gender, child-raising and the workplace needs to be part of a deeper project of economic justice. Crabb's essay is strong in its survey of the leading parental-leave schemes modelled in Scandinavia and by some of the big corporates in Australia. But if, as she argues, our own perceptions of gender roles are in urgent need of adjusting, we would do well to start by providing decent and equitable wages to those professionals who devote their time to caring for our young. One of the powerful things you realise as the parent of a newborn is the crucial importance of the "caring economy" that supports you. My partner and I wouldn't have survived those tricky early months of parenthood without friends and family. But equally important have been our cleaner, early childcare educators, local librarians and child health nurses. These are largely female-dominated and underpaid professions. For example, an astonishing 97 per cent of early childhood educators are women – some paid as little as $22 an hour.

Beyond the demands of child rearing, Crabb rightly points out the benefits of extending flexible work practices to all workers, regardless of whether they are parents. It is worth reflecting, however, on how we arrived at the point where the idea that workplaces should "flex" to accommodate the needs of self-fulfilment and nurture is seen as novel. The truth is that the neoliberal project of the last forty or so years has been brutally efficient at pricing all sorts of commodities while dangerously undervaluing a range of "externalities" (such as our warming climate). Blindness to the true cost of caring for the planet and ourselves is at the heart of the current economic order.

I wasn't surprised when Crabb's essay pointed to research finding that close to half of millennial men feel excluded from gender equality measures, and that men still tend to judge their worth by reference to their paid rather than caring work. Our political and economic systems create powerful norms that ripple through society to the level of the self. It's vitally important for millennials and others that we address the gender inequalities in our home and workplaces, but let's couple these efforts with the wider project of making the economy work for all of us.

Andrew Thackrah

Annabel Crabb

The first and best thing to say is that I've heard from a lot of men after publishing this essay. Like Tim Hammond, who returned home to Perth after quitting his job as an MP and was amazed at the number of men who sidled up to congratulate him in the street, I've been approached by men on the train, on social media, at the shops – even by a youngster who cycled past me in the street and wanted to let me know he was reading the Quarterly Essay.

When I wrote *The Wife Drought* in 2014, I got furtive responses from men. Like, I'd be sitting next to a bloke on a plane and about twenty minutes in he'd rustle his newspaper, cough and say, "My wife's reading your book." This time, the response is from men who've been reading it for themselves. The best day of the publicity tour was the lunch at the Melbourne Press Club where – at the back of the room – a couple of blokes hovered with their babies, employing the shallow knee-bend bouncing movement that very young children know to demand right at the moment their parent's meal has been served.

To a person who's spoken at hundreds of events, briefings, conferences, networking breakfasts and god knows what else about gender issues and become dully accustomed to the typical audience for such discussions (serried rows of interested eyes, a handbag under every chair), the presence of fathers and babies was a joyous development. Because the whole point of the essay was a gentle attempt at recognition from a female writer that the issues that crowd women's online forums – balancing work and life, parental guilt, the stress of juggling multiple deep and loving obligations – are *not just about us*.

There is room for men here. We have to make room, and they need to be permitted to occupy it. That is all.

It's so easy to arrange ourselves into predictable teams to duke out the gender-related controversies of our age. Easy, but stupid. (How did #MeToo ever become a men versus women thing, for example? Seems pretty obvious to me that it's a jerk versus non-jerk affair, dangly bits notwithstanding.)

We need, all of us, to be big enough to register the bigger picture. To step back and ignore our resentment or tiredness or anxiety and recognise that there are powerful forces and assumptions that regulate all of us, even those we might see as more fortunate than ourselves.

I'm indebted, as ever, to Marian Baird for her deep knowledge of Australia's reform history in this area, and to Andrew Wear, who is right to observe that the gender pay gap forces the hands of many heterosexual couples when making life decisions; both pieces of correspondence correct deficiencies in the essay, and I'm grateful for them.

Mark Tennant's account of domestic gatekeeping among women is an uncomfortable truth often avoided in the discussion about domestic workload; I wrote about it in *The Wife Drought* and welcome its inclusion in Professor Tennant's correspondence.

I loved Grant Marjoribanks' response, of course. It's always pleasant to be told that you've nailed it. But more, I loved his articulation of the inner life of a working father, prey to a remarkably similar constellation of guilt and uncertainty to that regularly described on women's chat-sites. We don't hear men's voices on this topic enough. Probably because we're not listening out for them; our dials are tuned to another station.

Speaking of which. Angela Shanahan's dial is tuned to expect feminists to whine about men and resent motherhood. Which is the only explanation for her mesmerising ability to read an entire 25,000-word essay without at any juncture, apparently, grasping the point of it. Determinedly, she describes the essay as a "long complaint" and adds a feline swipe at my level of devotion to the unglamorous elements of motherhood. For good measure, my "artfully recherché image" gets a whack too. (*What?*) I laughed out loud when I read that bit, because I was multitasking at the time; one hand scrolling through the text, the other administering a nit treatment to my own hair.

I'm pretty okay with the messy bits of motherhood, believe me. And I don't – this might come as a surprise to the correspondent in question – keep my children in child care until late hours, outsource their birthday parties, or get someone else to take them to the dentist. I changed the way I worked when I had kids. I shifted as much as I could – writing, editing – to after the kids' bedtimes and I worked from home whenever I could. I did different jobs: writing online and TV projects rather than the straight newspaper work that was my bread and butter. (I incorporated cooking into my work not – by the way – because I figured I could use a few ameliorative drops of 1950s housewife in the bitter cauldron-stew of my feminist PR image, but because I like to cook. Sometimes, Dr Freud, a cigar really is just a cigar.) Changing the way I worked was scary sometimes, and stressful too. But it was worth it. Being able to be with my children was the best part, but I also found the change stimulated me to look at things differently; I had more ideas, and better ones. And it's this great stuff on which fathers so often miss out.

I'm with Maddison Connaughton (whose response thrilled my heart): the mountainous terrain of Jennifer Baxter's graph describing the changes to a woman's life made by motherhood may be daunting, but the endless flatness of the men's graph evokes the tedium of a life from which something lively and urgent is missing. That's the point of the essay, really. It's not a whine about men. It's an attempt to see this issue in a different way. Rather than denigrating men for their failure to shoulder more responsibility at home, I wanted to look at the structural constraints that silently oblige men to keep doing what they do.

I would never question any family's decisions about how they want to manage things. Or argue that there should somehow be a mandated 50/50 split of domestic duties and breadwinning in every heterosexual couple so as to ensure gender parity. There are absolutely legitimate factors involved in such decisions: Who earns more? Whose job is more flexible? Whose career is at a point where a break or a change could be feasible or even helpful? Can we afford for one parent to be out of the workforce entirely?

But there are also other factors that are powerful for fathers at this life juncture. And they include: Men don't really take parental leave at my workplace. My parents/friends/co-workers will think it's weird if I take a year off. I'm worried that my work ethic will be questioned. And those are terrible reasons on which to base such a huge and intimate decision.

I didn't write this essay because I want a hand with the dishes. I'm blessed to be in a relationship with a man who works flexibly, does the laundry and doesn't need a list of instructions when in sole charge of our children, who we made together. I wrote it because I think it's absolutely absurd that children should miss out on their fathers, or vice versa, simply because some under-examined and outdated setting in our culture continues to suggest that working flexibly, or taking parental leave, is something really only intended for women to do. We used to think that being in the army, or being in the corner office, was something only men did, but we changed our minds about that over the years.

No reason we can't change our minds about this too.

Annabel Crabb

Marian Baird is professor of gender and employment relations at the University of Sydney. She was a key researcher and advocate for Australia's paid parental leave scheme, introduced in 2010.

Maddison Connaughton is the editor of *The Saturday Paper*.

Annabel Crabb is the ABC's chief online political writer. Her books include *Losing It*, *Rise of the Ruddbot* and *The Wife Drought*. She is the author of two Quarterly Essays, *Stop at Nothing: The Life and Adventures of Malcolm Turnbull* and *Men at Work: Australia's Parenthood Trap*.

Peter Hartcher is the political and international editor of *The Sydney Morning Herald*. His books include *Bubble Man*, *The Sweet Spot* and *To the Bitter End*. His first Quarterly Essay, *Bipolar Nation*, was published in 2007.

Grant Marjoribanks is a father and lawyer. He lives in Sydney with his wife and two children.

Angela Shanahan writes for *The Australian* and *The Spectator* (British and Australian editions), and formerly wrote for *The Sunday Telegraph*, *The Sydney Morning Herald* and *The Canberra Times*.

Mark Tennant is an emeritus professor in the Faculty of Arts and Social Sciences, University of Technology Sydney.

Andrew Thackrah is a working father with a PhD in Australian political history from the University of Western Australia.

Andrew Wear is a senior Australian public servant whose writing has appeared in academic journals, as well as in *The Mandarin* and *The Guardian*. His book *Solved!* will be published in 2020.

THE WORLD IS CHANGING, AND SO IS AUSTRALIA'S PLACE IN IT.

Australian Foreign Affairs, published three times a year, seeks to explore and encourage debate on significant developments affecting Australia and the region. Contributors are among Australia's top thinkers, including Paul Keating, Kim Beazley, Linda Jaivin, Allan Gyngell, George Megalogenis, Jennifer Rayner, Michael Wesley, Hugh White, Santilla Chingaipe and Christos Tsiolkas.

NEXT ISSUE – FEBRUARY 2020

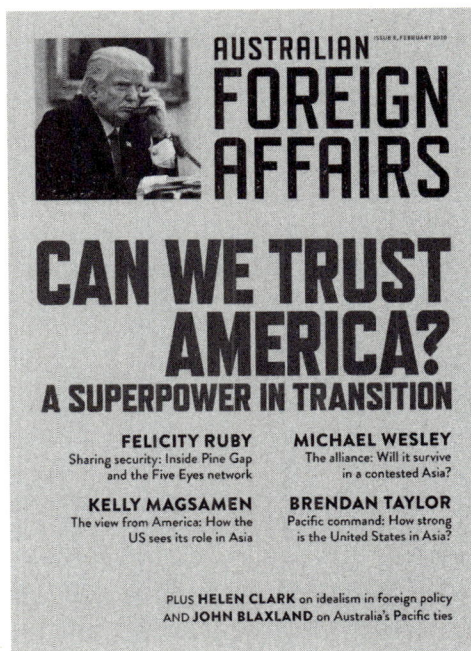

AUSTRALIAN FOREIGN AFFAIRS
OUR PLACE IN THE WORLD

Subscriptions from $29.99
australianforeignaffairs.com/subscribe

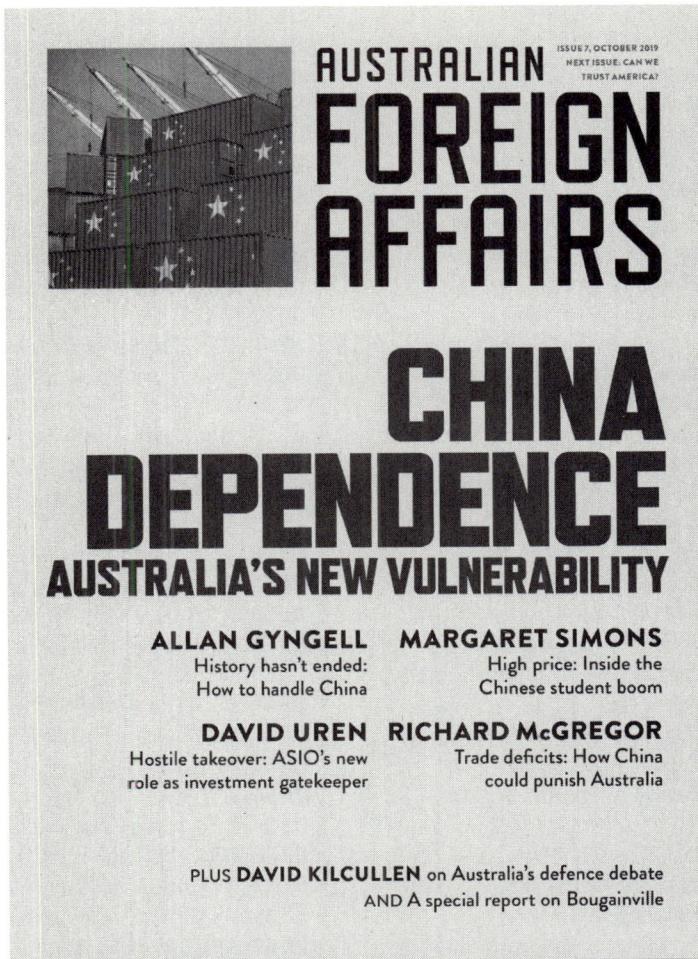

QUARTERLY ESSAY
BACK ISSUES

BACK ISSUES: (Prices include GST, postage and handling within Australia.) *Grey indicates out of stock.*

☐ QE 1 ($15.99) Robert Manne *In Denial*
☐ QE 2 ($15.99) John Birmingham *Appeasing Jakarta*
☐ QE 3 ($15.99) Guy Rundle *The Opportunist*
☐ QE 4 ($15.99) Don Watson *Rabbit Syndrome*
☐ QE 5 ($15.99) Mungo MacCallum *Girt By Sea*
☐ QE 6 ($15.99) John Button *Beyond Belief*
☐ QE 7 ($15.99) John Martinkus *Paradise Betrayed*
☐ QE 8 ($15.99) Amanda Lohrey *Groundswell*
☐ QE 9 ($15.99) Tim Flannery *Beautiful Lies*
☐ QE 10 ($15.99) Gideon Haigh *Bad Company*
☐ QE 11 ($15.99) Germaine Greer *Whitefella Jump Up*
☐ QE 12 ($15.99) David Malouf *Made in England*
☐ QE 13 ($15.99) Robert Manne with David Corlett *Sending Them Home*
☐ QE 14 ($15.99) Paul McGeough *Mission Impossible*
☐ QE 15 ($15.99) Margaret Simons *Latham's World*
☐ QE 16 ($15.99) Raimond Gaita *Breach of Trust*
☐ QE 17 ($15.99) John Hirst *'Kangaroo Court'*
☐ QE 18 ($15.99) Gail Bell *The Worried Well*
☐ QE 19 ($15.99) Judith Brett *Relaxed & Comfortable*
☐ QE 20 ($15.99) John Birmingham *A Time for War*
☐ QE 21 ($15.99) Clive Hamilton *What's Left?*
☐ QE 22 ($15.99) Amanda Lohrey *Voting for Jesus*
☐ QE 23 ($15.99) Inga Clendinnen *The History Question*
☐ QE 24 ($15.99) Robyn Davidson *No Fixed Address*
☐ QE 25 ($15.99) Peter Hartcher *Bipolar Nation*
☐ QE 26 ($15.99) David Marr *His Master's Voice*
☐ QE 27 ($15.99) Ian Lowe *Reaction Time*
☐ QE 28 ($15.99) Judith Brett *Exit Right*
☐ QE 29 ($15.99) Anne Manne *Love & Money*
☐ QE 30 ($15.99) Paul Toohey *Last Drinks*
☐ QE 31 ($15.99) Tim Flannery *Now or Never*
☐ QE 32 ($15.99) Kate Jennings *American Revolution*
☐ QE 33 ($15.99) Guy Pearse *Quarry Vision*
☐ QE 34 ($15.99) Annabel Crabb *Stop at Nothing*
☐ QE 35 ($15.99) Noel Pearson *Radical Hope*
☐ QE 36 ($15.99) Mungo MacCallum *Australian Story*
☐ QE 37 ($15.99) Waleed Aly *What's Right?*

☐ QE 38 ($15.99) David Marr *Power Trip*
☐ QE 39 ($15.99) Hugh White *Power Shift*
☐ QE 40 ($15.99) George Megalogenis *Trivial Pursuit*
☐ QE 41 ($15.99) David Malouf *The Happy Life*
☐ QE 42 ($15.99) Judith Brett *Fair Share*
☐ QE 43 ($15.99) Robert Manne *Bad News*
☐ QE 44 ($15.99) Andrew Charlton *Man-Made World*
☐ QE 45 ($15.99) Anna Krien *Us and Them*
☐ QE 46 ($15.99) Laura Tingle *Great Expectations*
☐ QE 47 ($15.99) David Marr *Political Animal*
☐ QE 48 ($15.99) Tim Flannery *After the Future*
☐ QE 49 ($15.99) Mark Latham *Not Dead Yet*
☐ QE 50 ($15.99) Anna Goldsworthy *Unfinished Business*
☐ QE 51 ($15.99) David Marr *The Prince*
☐ QE 52 ($15.99) Linda Jaivin *Found in Translation*
☐ QE 53 ($15.99) Paul Toohey *That Sinking Feeling*
☐ QE 54 ($15.99) Andrew Charlton *Dragon's Tail*
☐ QE 55 ($15.99) Noel Pearson *A Rightful Place*
☐ QE 56 ($15.99) Guy Rundle *Clivosaurus*
☐ QE 57 ($15.99) Karen Hitchcock *Dear Life*
☐ QE 58 ($15.99) David Kilcullen *Blood Year*
☐ QE 59 ($15.99) David Marr *Faction Man*
☐ QE 60 ($15.99) Laura Tingle *Political Amnesia*
☐ QE 61 ($15.99) George Megalogenis *Balancing Act*
☐ QE 62 ($15.99) James Brown *Firing Line*
☐ QE 63 ($15.99) Don Watson *Enemy Within*
☐ QE 64 ($15.99) Stan Grant *The Australian Dream*
☐ QE 65 ($15.99) David Marr *The White Queen*
☐ QE 66 ($15.99) Anna Krien *The Long Goodbye*
☐ QE 67 ($15.99) Benjamin Law *Moral Panic 101*
☐ QE 68 ($15.99) Hugh White *Without America*
☐ QE 69 ($15.99) Mark McKenna *Moment of Truth*
☐ QE 70 ($15.99) Richard Denniss *Dead Right*
☐ QE 71 ($15.99) Laura Tingle *Follow the Leader*
☐ QE 72 ($15.99) Sebastian Smee *Net Loss*
☐ QE 73 ($22.99) Rebecca Huntley *Australia Fair*
☐ QE 74 ($22.99) Erik Jensen *The Prosperity Gospel*
☐ QE 75 ($22.99) Annabel Crabb *Men at Work*

NAME:

ADDRESS:

EMAIL: PHONE:

Please include this form with payment details overleaf.

☐ **ONE-YEAR AUTO-RENEWING PRINT AND DIGITAL SUBSCRIPTION: $69.95***
  REQUIRES EMAIL & CREDIT CARD, 4 issues, save 24% off the cover price

☐ **TWO-YEAR PRINT AND DIGITAL SUBSCRIPTION: $149.95** 8 issues

☐ **ONE-YEAR AUTO-RENEWING PRINT AND DIGITAL INTERNATIONAL SUBSCRIPTION: $109.95***
  REQUIRES EMAIL & CREDIT CARD, 4 issues

☐ **ONE-YEAR DIGITAL ONLY SUBSCRIPTION: $49.95** REQUIRES EMAIL, 4 issues

☐ **ONE-YEAR PRINT AND DIGITAL GIFT SUBSCRIPTION: $79.95** 4 issues, save 13% off the cover
  price. Subscriptions outside Australia $119.95

☐ **TWO-YEAR PRINT AND DIGITAL GIFT SUBSCRIPTION** $149.95 8 issues, save 13% off the cover
  price

☐ TICK HERE TO COMMENCE SUBSCRIPTION WITH THE CURRENT ISSUE

SUBSCRIBER'S NAME:

ADDRESS:

EMAIL: PHONE:

RECIPIENT'S NAME:

ADDRESS:

EMAIL: PHONE:

PAYMENT DETAILS: Enclose a cheque/money order made out to Schwartz Books Pty Ltd.
Or debit my credit card (MasterCard, Visa and Amex accepted).
Freepost: Quarterly Essay, Reply Paid 90094, Carlton VIC 3053
All prices include GST, postage and handling.

CARD NO. ☐☐☐☐ ☐☐☐☐ ☐☐☐☐ ☐☐☐☐

EXPIRY DATE: /   CCV: AMOUNT: $

PURCHASER'S NAME: SIGNATURE:

PURCHASER'S EMAIL:

Subscribe online at **quarterlyessay.com/subscribe** • Freecall: 1800 077 514 • Phone: 03 9486 0288
Email: subscribe@quarterlyessay.com (please do not send electronic scans of this form)

---

* Your subscription will automatically renew until you notify us to stop. Prior to the end of your subscription period, we will
   send you a reminder notice that will indicate the renewal price. If you do not notify us to stop the renewal, your credit or debit
   card will automatically be charged for the same period. You may notify us to stop the renewal via the account dashboard or by
   contacting us. Australian subscriptions only.

WANT THE LATEST FROM QUARTERLY ESSAY?

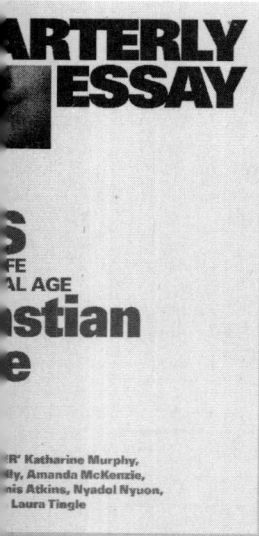

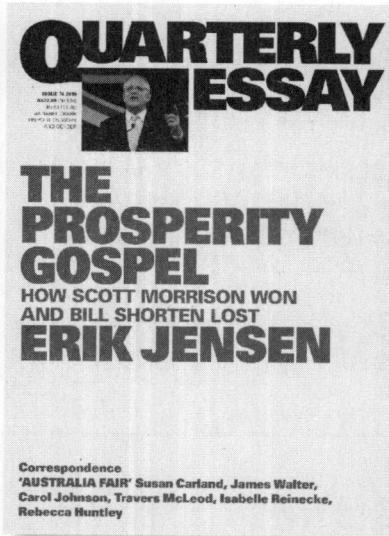

QUARTERLY ESSAY

THE PROSPERITY GOSPEL
HOW SCOTT MORRISON WON AND BILL SHORTEN LOST
ERIK JENSEN

Correspondence
'AUSTRALIA FAIR' Susan Carland, James Walter,
Carol Johnson, Travers McLeod, Isabelle Reinecke,
Rebecca Huntley

QUARTERLY ESSAY

MEN AT WORK
AUSTRALIA'S PARENTHOOD TRAP
ANNABEL CRABB

Correspondence
'THE PROSPERITY GOSPEL' James Newton, David Marr,
Judith Brett, Barry Jones, Elizabeth Flux, Kristina Keneally,
Patrick Mullins, Matthew Ricketson, Russell Marks,
Erik Jensen

**Subscribe to the Friends of Quarterly Essay
newsletter to receive important updates on
future editions, as well as exclusive offers,
news and events.**

quarterlyessay.com.au